# Faithfully
## DEPLOYING THE SPIRIT OF SERVANTHOOD

♦

Service to God, Pastors and Ministry
is the Heart of Servanthood

Ferdinard S. Lawson

**Multi-Award Winning Author**

First Published by
Hetura Books Co. Ltd.
ARS – Boundary Road, Ogbojo;
Hse No. OG17/1, East Legon; Accra.
info@heturabooks.com
www.heturabooks.com

+233 (0)307-001-724
+233 (0)233-507-447

Copyright © by Ferdinand Senyo Lawson, 2017
All rights reserved

ISBN:1519667655

For your personal copy of this book, information about other books by the author or bulk purchase, please contact the author on 00447490738849 or
www.ferdinardlawson.com;
info@ferdinardlawson.com

All rights reserved. No part of this book may be reproduced, stored in a retrieval system, transmitted in any form, or by any means, electronic, mechanical, photocopying, recording, or otherwise, without the prior written permission of the author, or his legal representative(s).

Unless otherwise stated, all Scripture verses are from the King James Version (KJV) of the Holy Bible.

This book is affectionately dedicated to my deceased grandmother, **Madam Felicia Ami Ocloo,** who never gave up on me but dedicated her life time to introduce me to my maker (GOD). Grandma, thank you and May your soul continue to rest with God. Introducing me to Jesus Christ, was the best gift you have left with me.

## ACKNOWLEDGEMENTS

First and foremost, I would like to thank God and the Holy Spirit for the love, inspiration and assistance in the discovery of my purpose in life. Without the Holy Spirit, I wouldn't have served faithfully in my office as an Armour Bearer.

Your grace has been sufficient for me during those periods of service. Thank you for leading and guiding my writing of this book to contribute to the building of your Kingdom.

My sincere gratitude goes to my spiritual mentor, Pastor Charles Owusu (Deeper Christian Life Bible Church. Ghana), who I first served faithfully and in loyalty as an armour bearer back in my youthful days in Ghana for many years. You are a great inspiration to me and my family both here in United Kingdom and Ghana. God bless you.

I express my profound gratitude to Rev. Dr Paul Yaw Frimpong-Manso (General Superintendent of the General Council of Assemblies of God, Ghana), for his prayers and encouragement to bring this book to reality. May God richly bless you.

To Bishop Dr. Julius K. Owusu-Ansah, words cannot express my gratitude to the committee for your support, kindness, prayer and encouragement. You dedicated your time in writing the foreword for this book simply because you believed in the information and the revelations in it. Few words are only used to describe great men like you. Thank you for the seed you have sown into my life. God bless you.

To all my teachers in life, mentors and more who have taught me how to live a positive life, your thoughts, words and ideas have truly shaped me for my generation especially to those who I have served with all my heart. May God reward you according to your works.

My wife, Deborah and my children (Joshua and Jessica), words cannot express how much I love you. Your laughter and love have always stirred me for newer heights in life. Serving as an armour bearer would not have been possible without your support, motivation, encouragement, and prayers. You never complained when I had to leave you alone with Prince and Princess from the day they were born in order for me to serve. May God restore and reward you for the sacrifices you made for me to serve faithfully and in loyalty.

To my parents, MR and MRS Lawson, and my siblings, God bless you so much for the foundation of education and training you gave me during my formative years. May God continue to keep you alive to reap the fruits of your hard work. Your labour shall not be in vain.

To my parents-in-law, especially His Excellency Mr. Justice Joseph B. Akamba; you instilled in me the idea to turn my knowledge into articles. I can gratefully say that they are now in books. I want to say thank you so much for being an inspiration. God bless you.

# CONTENTS

Dedication..................................................................iii

Acknowledgements.....................................................v

Foreword....................................................................ix

Introduction............................................................xiii

**Chapter One**     Responsibilities Of An
                    Armour Bearer..........................................1

**Chapter Two**     Cultivating The Fruit Of
                    The Spirit...............................................39

**Chapter Three**   Independent Spirit: Avoid It
                    At All Cost..............................................61

**Chapter Four**    Have A Purpose In Life
                    As An Armor-Bearer................................67

**Chapter Five**    Don't Entertain Discouragers
                    Around Your Ministry.............................77

**Chapter Six**     Free Your Mind From
                    Negative Thoughts..................................83

**Chapter Seven**   Dwell On The Word Of God Daily..........89

**Chapter Eight**   Trust In The Lord In The
                    Face Of Challenges.................................97

| | | |
|---|---|---|
| **Chapter Nine** | Maintain The Spirit Of Thanksgiving | 105 |
| **Chapter Ten** | Don't Give Up On Your Ministry | 117 |
| **Chapter Eleven** | Stay Away From Toxic Relationships | 125 |
| **Chapter Twelve** | Catch Your Pastor's Spirit | 135 |
| **Chapter Thirteen** | Don't Deny Your Ministry Your Invaluable Input | 147 |

Conclusion..............................................................................155

References.............................................................................157

Prayer Guide For Your Church
And Pastor By Dr. Richard J. Krejcir.....................................159

# FOREWORD

Ferdinard Senyo Lawson is a prolific writer who writes with the mind-set of Christ. He has been commissioned to equip and edify the body of Christ to function effectively and efficiently.

May the Holy Spirit download the contents of this exciting and fascinating book into your spirit and you shall never be the same.

May God activate the latent and dormant 'potency' in you into an optimised potential as you explore the pages of this book.

This book shall transform your thinking and enhance your performance to serve in absolute humility.

You shall be exposed to some of the deeper truths of the Sacred Word. Many books are replicate of what others have written. But I can guarantee you, Faithfully Deploying the Spirit of Servanthood, is an original manual from the third heavens.

The author's style of writing is unique and insightful. Many pastors have died as paupers without realising and actualising their visions. Their visions couldn't be translated into realities. Why? The devil was able to use the flock to frustrate, suppress and destroy their destinies. Fragmentation, proliferation and mushrooming of churches in our contemporary era are disheartening and a worrying trend – this book is an antidote.

It tells you about positioning yourself in the body of Christ in order to be used by God to help your ministry. Not all of us are called to be pastors, yet you can function effectively by being the armour-bearer of your pastor; thus serving with dedication, joy and humility. All have been called to serve.

Whether by design or default, the church has produced Christian workers with chip on their shoulders – ARROGANCE. The book emphasises the need for a paradigm shift if a meaningful breakthrough is to be achieved. This book seeks to address the anomaly for the 'Corpus Christi'. It is a must-read book.

I humbly recommend it as a manual to all pastors and Christian workers. It must be taught at the children's Sunday school up to the adult section. Bible colleges, seminaries and theological institutions should recommend it to their students as text books.

We need a unified, solid and triumphant church to take 'Captivity Captive'.

It is often asked, 'Who watches the watchman?' Then 'Who pastors the pastor?' Yes! It is God. But you are God's agent of help to your pastor.

2 Samuel 18:3 brings the import of the book vividly. "But the people answered, Thou shall not go forth… but now thou art worth ten thousand of us; therefore now it is better that thou succour us out of the city". David as a leader was prevented from engaging in further warfare as he was aging. A leader must be protected at all cost for his worth cannot be quantified.

Luke 15:18-19 says, "And I am no more worthy to be called thy son, make me as one of thy hired servants." As children of God, we need to consciously and voluntarily recognise ourselves as servants. Servanthood is by choice.

Bro. Ferdinard is a man of integrity who carries the mantle of servanthood in his generation. He is an unassuming young man who is pregnant with the Word. We love him for producing such an exquisite and classic work. It is a masterpiece.

As you read this book, I commend you to the grace of God which is able to establish and make you whole and perfect. May God not withhold any good thing from you.

I decree and declare the sufficiency of Christ upon your life. As I foreword this book, I pray that my service to the body of Christ shall be satisfactory, appreciable and acceptable in Jesus name. Shalom!

**Bishop Dr. Julius K. Owusu – Ansah**

*Founder and Leader* of C.B.C Int.; *Founder and President* of International Fellowship of Bishops and Apostles; *Faculty Board Chairman* of World-Wide Bible Institute

## TIPS FOR HAPPINESS AND VITALITY

1. A SMILE is good for your face and health.
2. At least 20 minutes of exercise, three times a week.
3. Drink at least eight glasses of water per day.
4. Don't withhold your urinary bladder; empty it as soon as possible.
5. Emptying the bowels is good for the body function.
6. Beware of herbal drugs. Drugs sold in vehicles should be avoided. Consult your physician before taking them.
7. Avoid buying drugs from the counter. Early detection of an illness is good for its cure.
8. Beware of the unprescribed intake of food supplements. They are good but consult your doctor before taking them.
9. Eat well. A balanced diet is good for your health.
10. Have enough rest. Sleep well. At least six to seven hours of continuous sleep.
11. Ante-natal care is the first step for a safe delivery.
12. Fasting is good. Don't fast when you are seriously ill.

May God give you the grace to live well.

Produced by Bishop Dr. Julius

# INTRODUCTION

Are you a born again and are you actually a Christian? Then you are called to do the work of ministry. You don't need any title to work in your Father's house as a Christian. You may find yourself in the ushering department, children class department, sound and media department, evangelism and soul-winning department, and so on and so forth. These are all ministries within the church that we need to take seriously and be faithful till the Lord comes.

Every Christian must or should be equipped to serve in one capacity or the other in their church. It is the duty of the pastor or leader of the church to identify the needs in the church and where everyone can function. The leadership of the church should take full responsibility to ensure that any vacancy in the church is filled. It is also important that every church member is encouraged, helped, motivated and equipped where necessary to get involved in the work of ministry.

Ministry is not limited to the pulpit. Ministry goes beyond preaching behind the pulpit, laying on of hands, and singing. It is very vital that every church member is equipped to function in their church using their various gifts and talents to contribute to the growth of the church. A service rendered to fellow men is a service to God. I have personally discovered that many members are sitting in the church with great professional qualifications which the body of Christ can benefit from but because of some insecurity from the leadership of some churches, these individuals just come and warm the benches thinking that, they are not needed to play or contribute to the growth or the development of the church. Some even limit their contribution to tithe and offering simply because that has been the focus of the leadership.

Every church, be it local or national, has more needs that must be attended to. These needs cannot be met unless many members are equipped to do the work of ministry. We are all called to serve God, our ministry and our pastors in the area of serving in one capacity or the other. You can serve by offering yourself in the area of teaching Sunday school, mentoring the youth ministry of your church, visiting church members admitted in hospital, helping the widows and the orphans, being responsible for sending birthday cards on behalf of the church, among others.

What amazes me is the fact that we have many books on leadership but very few of those have been written on servanthood. You will be very surprised to know the number of people trying so hard to get into leadership as compared to the ones desiring to be servants in ministry.

One can serve God through serving their community and helping out to clean the streets, share food to the homeless, etc. These can easily be done through charitable events, play groups and so on. We are commanded to be the light and salt of the world. The only way our lights can be seen and our salt tasted is when we are fully equipped to do the work of ministry.

During my 18 years of serving God and seven years of serving as the Senior Armour Bearer to Bishop Michael Hutton-Wood of House of Judah Praise Ministry (United Kingdom), I came to appreciate the importance of an armour bearer in a pastor's life. The question is; who is an armour bearer in a pastor's life?

A pastor's armour bearer is a committed church member who has been elected, chosen or appointed by the head pastor based on good report and dedication to see to the successful execution of the work of God through the hands of the pastor. The pastor's armour bearer's duty is to be a faithful and loyal servant. Their service is purely based on a deeper love for God's Kingdom.

A pastor's armour bearer is an individual who has dedicated his life to serve the pastor and be his or her right hand man/woman and providing support and encouragement for them. A pastor's armour bearer is the one who is sold out completely for the assignment of the pastor's vision and mandate, demonstrating and displaying a godly character or attitude of faith in standing with the pastor.

An armour bearer is the individual Christian in the church who is chosen by the pastor because of his or her integrity, faithfulness, loyalty to service, and also because of his or her stance for the Word and the work of God by demonstrating the spirit of bravery to stand by the pastor and the ministry (CHURCH) especially during challenging moments.

## You cannot have the anointing of Elisha until you have served Elijah!

The spirit of submission is one of the greatest characters demanded from a pastor's armour bearer. Any individual who is not prepared to be submissive to the pastor he or she serves is not permitted to be called an armour bearer. A pastor's armour bearer must be willing and ready to be submissive to their pastors, to the church members, and above all to GOD.

The rod of the pastor you don't value and serve faithfully can never work in your hands.

> "Then he called quickly to the young man, his armour bearer, and said to him, 'Draw your sword and kill me, so that it will not be said of me, 'A woman slew him.'" So the young man pierced him through, and he died"
>
> **Judges 9:54 NIV ©1984**
>
> "Jonathan said to his young armour-bearer, 'Come, let's go over to the outpost of those uncircumcised fellows. Perhaps the LORD will act in our behalf. Nothing can hinder the LORD from saving, whether by many or by few'"
>
> **1 Samuel 14:6 NIV ©1984**

Additionally, a pastor's armour bearer is the individual who sacrifices his wills and desires so as to walk in togetherness or agreement, through total submission to the leader who has spiritual authority over his/her life (Romans 13:12). Submit to him as to Jesus. Is it possible to submit to God and refuse to submit to His delegated authority over your life?

It is very important that as an armour bearer, we view obedience to our pastors not only as men but serve and obey them as unto the Lord and the spiritual authority they walk and operate in. I have come to realise that our Heavenly Father will never establish us as armour bearers until we discover how to be submissive to spiritual authorities placed over us (1 Peter 2:20).

As you begin to read this book, may the Holy Spirit himself give you the knowledge and insight to develop the right spirit and sacrifice to serve your pastors as a true son or daughter and an armour bearer.

May you not collapse when things appear impossible or busier but you will develop the spirit and the sacrifices of Jonathan, Joshua and Elisha to stand with your pastor to fulfil God's mandate for His church. Be empowered as you stand with your pastors through COMMITMENT, FAITHFULNESS, LOYALTY, and HUMILITY AND SACRIFICE TO SERVICE.

BE BLESSED AND EMPOWERED IN JESUS NAME.

# Chapter One

◆

# RESPONSIBILITIES OF AN ARMOUR BEARER

◆

Responsibility can be defined as an act of carrying out a duty or an obligation that is assigned to an individual which he or she is required to fulfil wholeheartedly. Therefore in the context of an armour bearer, it is the responsibility of him or her to carry out duties assigned to him/her by his/her pastor. An armour bearer is a servant to the pastor and the ministry. He/she carries an additional duty within the church to ensure that the workload of the pastor is lessened.

From the Old Testament, we discovered that most armour-bearers were servants who carried additional weapons for commanders. This was evident in the life of Abimelech (Judges 9:54), Saul (1 Samuel 16:12), Jonathan (1 Samuel 14:6-17), and Joab (2 Samuel 18:15). You will also discover that an armour-bearer's duty is to kill or fight his master's enemies and after a long time, some of David's armour-bearers were no longer mentioned (1 Kings 12:18; 20:33). An armour bearer can be regarded as a pastor's body guard.

Therefore, this raises the question as to what the main roles or duties are of an armour bearer in a pastor's life. The main roles or responsibilities of a pastor's armour bearer is to serve in the capacity of attending to the needs of; caring and helping the pastor to promote, motivate, and push his/her vision for the church.

> "And he gave some, apostles; and some, prophets; and some, evangelists; and some, pastors and teachers; For the perfecting of the saints, for the work of the ministry, for the edifying of the body of Christ."
>
> **Ephesians 4:12 KJV**

Every pastor's armour bearer is commanded to operate by the leading of the Holy Spirit as to develop the character, faithfulness, loyalty, and mentality of servanthood like that of King David's mighty men, Elisha and Joshua, Gehazi, Stephen and Phillip. Therefore this actually makes it very important that there is a great demand for pastors' armour bearers who will bear the arms of their pastors through selfless service unto God and His servants (PASTORS).

## DUTY 1: KNOW YOUR PASTORS

> "And we beseech you, brethren, to know them which labour among you, and are over you in the Lord, and admonish you; And to esteem them very highly in love

for their work's sake. [And] be at peace among yourselves"

**1 Thessalonians 5:12**

Knowing your pastors is to consciously study them, observe them, and imitate them as they imitate Christ. The pastor becomes your standard by which you live your life because they imitate CHRIST.

Knowing your pastor does not only mean to be in their face 24/7, or invite them for parties or dinner in a restaurant. It means to develop the spirit to connect and reason with them. As much as taking and inviting them to parties and special occasions are needed; knowing them goes beyond all that.

We were told in 1 Thessalonians 5:13 to 'esteem them highly in love'. Loving and respecting them places you at a greater pedestal to knowing your pastors. Personally, having served for many years under my bishop, I have realised that our relationship with men of God (PASTORS) is key. I have also discovered that the more I spent time with bishop and shared things with him, the more I understood and knew him for myself. This means that until I determined to relate and know my pastor, I would not be able to understand him.

If you know how your television works, you do not struggle to use it. The same applies with knowing your pastors. You can only receive and benefit from them fully when you know how they operate. This however means that as you follow your pastors very well as he follows Jesus, you are also made.

In every relationship, when one party refuses to relate well to the other party, the relationship breaks down. If you are not prepared and ready to invest into knowing your pastors' heart and how they operate, then I can assure you that you are not ready to be called to be an armour bearer yet.

> "The amount of God's anointing current flowing into your life depends on your connectivity to your pastor."
>
> **Ferdinard S. Lawson**

So as an armour bearer never get to the point to say that your current is greater than the generator (pastor). When you get to know your pastors, it makes it easier for you to live at peace with them. Do never get angry with them and decide to leave the church. Be planted in the church and use all your gifts to add value to the place. Do never leave a fruitful and healthy relationship even when, sometimes, you do not agree with some behavioural traits and character.

Until you remain planted in that soil (church), you cannot flourish (Psalm 1:1-3). No matter what happens to you in that church, remain steadfast, work and serve your pastor with respect; and the Lord God will reward your faithfulness in due season.

From the above passage, we read that it is very necessary to know our pastors and relate with the accordingly because of their labour to and for the children of God especially through the sharing of God's Word, praying and watching over our soul, and so forth. It

> **The levels of relationship and submission you have with your pastor determine the level of grace and honour that comes on you.**
>
> FERDINARD S. LAWSON

is a shame that many armour bearers work around their pastors but have not really known them, let alone catch their spirit. The Word of God says that, 'Know them', and knowing them comes through personal and spiritual intimacy with them. You cannot relate well and function effectively without knowing your pastors. This is what makes you different from the rest of the flock (church members). The disciples were able to change the world because they knew Jesus and had personal relationship with him especially, Peter (John 13:23).

## DUTY 2: PRAY FOR YOUR PASTORS (HEAD)

2 Thessalonians 3:1-2 reads, "Finally, brothers, pray for us that the message of the Lord may spread rapidly and be honoured, just as it was with you. And pray that we may be delivered from wicked and evil men, for not everyone has faith."

> "For we (pastors) wrestle not against flesh and blood, but against principalities, against power of rulers of darkness of this world, against spiritual wickedness in high places."
>
> **Ephesians 6:12**

God has a master plan and purpose for all pastors and the enemies (devils) are doing things possible to frustrate them. The devil's agenda is to defocus your pastor. That is why you as an armour bearer need to devout a special time to pray for your pastors. Stand in the gap to intercede for the ministry because the evil ones are not relaxing at all but working overtime to bring pastors down. The enemy will not sit down to drink hot chocolate because many souls are won into the Kingdom of

God but will attack you from all angles just to derail or abort the vision of God upon their family and ministry.

The enemies of progress will set in to frustrate your pastors' hard work and their perseverance to the assignment of God.

"And they came to the chief priests and elders, and said, we have bound ourselves under a great curse, that we will eat nothing until we have slain Paul." Acts 23:14

The devil knows how powerful your pastors will be when prayers are made for them. So as an armour bearer, it is your first point of duty to fortify yourself with prayer daily against any forms of attack that the devil will wage against your pastors.

> "The anointing on your pastor will not attract butterflies but will attract bees."
> **FERDINAND S. LAWSON**

The good news is that God has given us (armour bearers) the power of prayer which we can engage anytime and anywhere to destroy the works of the enemies that try to limit our pastors and the ministry.

One thing I have discovered as an armour bearer is that the devil fears a prayerful person because prayer is the weapon in the life of a believer. Our pastors can live above satanic limitations and preach and function greatly only if you (armour bearer) engage in prayer. Prayer breaks the shackles of the enemies and sets pastors free from the attacks of evil ones. Prayer is the act of pleading fervently or asking and seeking God's face for something with intense yearning.

"Pray without ceasing"

**1 Thessalonians 5:17**

"And from the days of John the Baptist until now the kingdom of heaven suffered violence, and the violent take it by force"

**Matthew 11:12 KJV**

Let me tell you a story that was told by C. Peter Wagner of an incident that took place on an airliner. For the purpose of this example, all names are changed. I will call the believer (KAFUI) and the devil agent (MR. SHAME). On this particular flight, Kafui who was a Christian and a devoted believer was sitting next to another handsome man (Mr. Shame) in the business class. During the course of the flight, Kafui noticed that Mr. Shame had bowed his head and moving his lips as if he was praying.

When Mr. Shame had finished his so-called prayer, Kafui thought he was also a believer and a Christian because of the prayer posture. So Kafui engaged in conversations with him and asked him if he was a pastor or intercessor. Mr. Shame replied astonishingly that he was actually an agent of the devil with an assignment to bring about the fall of believers especially pastors and their families who are on the mission for the Lord and leading sinners to the Lord. He went on to say that he was sent to put limitations before all pastors and their ministries in order to bring carnality and immorality, worldliness and backsliding in the lives of church members.

Additionally, his main agenda is to frustrate believers in the area of business, education, marriage, finances, church and ministry. Through these, he would derail them from getting to their sure destiny and to heaven.

After that short conversation, Mr. Shame went back to his posture to ensure that his main purpose on the plane and the place he was going was materialised. In fact, the encounter made Kafui to realise how crucial and powerful prayer is in the journey of life. The devil's agenda is to put limits, blockages, and pains in your pastors' lives to strike them from God's purposes.

"Strike the shepherd and the sheep scatter"

**Zechariah 13:7**

As an armour bearer, you need to know that the devil targets leaders (pastors) because he knows that if he can destroy them, he can destroy churches possibly your entire generation (family). In Hosea 12:13, we are told that, "And by a prophet the LORD brought Israel out of Egypt, and by a prophet was he preserved."

The condition of pastors eventually affects the condition and the atmosphere of the church. Do you know that a tired and burnt-out pastor greatly affects the spirit of the church members and in turn makes the sheep to scatter? A pastor who becomes immoral due to lack of discipline and the attack of the enemies derails and slows down the spirit of God in a church. This is the reason why as an armour bearer, you never stop praying for your pastor to remain closer to God and to keep receiving manna from heaven for the whole church because any pastor who has lost intimacy with God will begin to live in the flesh and will end up living a life of impurity.

Armour bearers should cultivate the habit of praying for their pastors so that the devil doesn't derail them.

Nobody knows how much attack pastors encounter and the level at which they need our prayers. You may not actually know the kind of evil plans and experiences that the devil puts in your pastors' lives just to make them quit the work of God.

That is why as an armour bearer, you need to allocate and dedicate some quality time to intercede and pray for your pastors because the evil ones are not sleeping and snoring. They are working overtime to see them fall, derail, die, lose the zeal and passion for souls.

> "Prayer is what it takes to bring heavenly resources to meet the needs on earth."
>
> W.F. KUMUYI
> (DEEPER LIFE BIBLE CHURCH)

It is prayer that puts God to work on your behalf. Prayer puts your angels to work and fight the invisible enemies against your church and the leadership (pastors).

A time came in Solomon's life that he needed to hear from God concerning the purpose and the direction for his life. He went to God in prayer to enquire of God's plan for him. In 11 Chronicles 7:12-15, we discovered that "And the Lord appeared to Solomon by night and said unto him, I have heard your prayer and have chosen this place myself, for a house of sacrifice..." When you read on you will see that Solomon offered his sacrifice at the appointed place. Divine instruction and direction is what your pastors get from God when you engage in the power of prayer for them.

According to Michael Fackerell, if you desire to see miraculous results in your pastors' life and your church, then you need to engage in effective prayer and fasting for them. Remember that you as an armour bearer become an agent of God when you engage in prayer daily. You become a representative of your pastor before the Kingdom of God to bring His purpose into fruition in the life of men and women in the church and your pastors.

> "And pray for us, too, that God may open a door for our message, so that we may proclaim the mystery of Christ, for which I am in chains. Pray that I may proclaim it clearly, as I should"
>
> **Colossians 4:3-4**
>
> "Finally, brothers, pray for us that the message of the Lord may spread rapidly and be honoured, just as it was with you. And pray that we may be delivered from wicked and evil men, for not everyone has faith"
>
> **2 Thessalonians 3:1-2**

While there are many things one could pray for pastors, as an armour bearer, here are five straightforward scriptural reasons why pastors need your prayers.

## 1. PRAY FOR THEIR SPIRITUAL PROTECTION FROM THE WORLD, THE FLESH AND THE DEVIL

Whether it was Moses' sinful anger leading to his striking of the rock (Numbers 20:7-12), David's adultery and murder (2 Samuel

11), or Simon Peter's denial of the Lord (Matthew 26:69-75) and practical denial of justification by faith alone (Galatians 2:11-21), ministers are faced with the reality of the weakness of the flesh, the assaults of the world and the rage of the devil.

There have been a plethora of ministers who have fallen into sinful practices in the history of the church and so brought disgrace to the name of Christ. Since Satan has ministers of the gospel (and their families) locked in his sight – and since God's honour is at stake in a heightened sense with any public ministry of the Word, members of the church should pray that their pastor and their pastor's family would not fall prey to the world, the flesh, or the devil.

## 2. PRAY FOR THEIR DELIVERANCE FROM THE PHYSICAL ATTACKS OF THE WORLD AND THE DEVIL

While under prison guard in Rome, the apostle Paul encouraged the believers in Philippi to pray for his release when he wrote, "I know that this will turn out for my deliverance through your prayer and the supply of the Spirit of Jesus Christ" (Philippians 1:19). (See also 2 Corinthians 1:9-11). When Herod imprisoned Simon Peter, we learnt that "constant prayer was offered to God for him by the church" (Acts 12:5). After an exodus-like deliverance from prison, Luke tells us that Peter showed up at the home where the disciples were continuing to pray for his deliverance. This is yet another example of the minister being delivered from harm due, in part, to the prayers of the saints.

## 3. PRAY FOR DOORS TO BE OPENED TO THEM FOR THE SPREAD OF THE GOSPEL

In his letter to the Colossians, Paul asked the church to be praying "that God would open to us a door for the Word, to speak the mystery of Christ for which I am also in chains" (Colossians 4:3). The success of the spread of the gospel is dependent in part on the prayers of the people of God. This way, the church shares in the gospel ministry with the pastor. Though he is not the only one in the body who is called to spread the Word, he has a unique calling to "do the work of an evangelist." The saints help him fulfil this work by praying that the Lord would open doors "for the Word, to speak the mystery of Christ."

### 4. PRAY THAT THEY MIGHT HAVE BOLDNESS AND POWER TO PREACH THE GOSPEL

In addition to praying for open doors for the ministry of the Word, the people of God should pray that ministers would have Spirit-wrought boldness. When writing to the church in Ephesus, the apostle Paul asked them to pray for him "that utterance may be given to me, that I may open my mouth boldly to make known the mystery of the gospel" (Ephesians 6:19).

There is a well-known story of several college students going to visit the Metropolitan Tabernacle in order to hear Charles Spurgeon preach. As the story goes, Spurgeon met them at the door and offered to show them around. At one point he asked if they wanted to see the church's heater plant (boiler room). He took them downstairs where they saw hundreds of people praying for God's blessings on the service and on Spurgeon's preaching. The gathering of the people of God to pray for the ministry of the Word is what he called "the heating plant!" Believers can help ministers by praying that they would be given boldness and power in preaching the gospel.

## 5. PRAY THAT THEY MIGHT HAVE A SPIRIT OF WISDOM AND UNDERSTANDING

One of the most pressing needs for a minister of the gospel is that he would be given the necessary wisdom to counsel, to know when to confront, to mediate and to discern the particular pastoral needs of a congregation. This is an all-encompassing and a recurring need. The minister is daily faced with particular challenges for which he desperately needs the wisdom of Christ. It is said of Jesus that, "the Spirit of wisdom and knowledge and of counsel and might" was upon Him (Isaiah 11:2).

Servants of Christ need that same Spirit. Much harm is done to the church as a whole if the minister does not proceed with the wisdom commensurate to the challenges with which he is faced. Those who benefit from this wisdom can help the minister by calling down this divine blessing from heaven upon him.

> "And pray for us, too, that God may open a door for our message, so that we may proclaim the mystery of Christ, for which I am in chains"
>
> **Colossians 4:3-4**

In Ephesians 6:19-20, we read, "Pray also for me, that whenever I open my mouth, words may be given me so that I will fearlessly make known the mystery of the gospel, for which I am an ambassador in chains. Pray that I may declare it fearlessly, as I should."

Every armour bearer should have this in mind to pray for their pastor so that they can preach the Word of God boldly. Pray that God will continue to maintain peace and harmony in the church.

## DUTY 3: HONOUR YOUR PASTORS

"Honour your father and mother, (which is the first commandment with a promise), so that it may be well with you, and that you may live long on the earth"

**Ephesians 6:2-3**

Therefore what do I mean by honouring your pastors? To honour actually means to value, respect and obey them, etc. When you look in the Bible, you will understand that honour has been defined differently. For example, the Bible regards honour as having value, weight, splendour and glory for somebody and seeing or esteeming them so highly for the office they carry. That means that to honour your pastor is to value their knowledge, wisdom, and their personalities in the spiritual office they operate in.

In the eyes of God, there is no time limit where an armour bearer can get and wouldn't have to honour their pastors again. The same way we do not have to choose a biological parent to honour and respect them, we do not have to decide when we should honour our pastors.

The Bible made it clear in 2 Chronicles 20:20b that, "Believe in the WORD of the Lord your God, and believe in His law, and believe in His prophets; and ye shall prosper." This means that we have the responsibility as armour bearers to ensure that we honour our pastors because our prosperity depends on how we honour and respect them.

"And by a prophet the LORD brought Israel out of Egypt, and by a prophet was he preserved"

**Hosea 12:13**

Our preservation and protection is based on how we treat and honour our pastors. This indicates that when it comes to honouring our pastors, it is not conditional based upon how good the pastors are in preaching, speaking, socialising or how good looking and beautiful they appear or look, or what kinds of home they were brought up in. It is not in their body sizes. God expects us to honour our pastors unconditionally simply because they are our spiritual parents and they watch over us.

"And He gave some, apostles; and some, prophets; and some, evangelists; and some, pastors and teachers; For the perfecting of the saints, for the work of the ministry, for the edifying of the body of Christ: Till we all come in the unity of the faith, and of the knowledge of the Son of God, unto a perfect man, unto the measure of the stature of the fullness of Christ"

**Ephesians 4:11-13**

It may sound very hard to understand that you as an armour bearer are to honour your pastors even if you think they don't deserve it, simply because they are your parents. I have come to appreciate that when you honour your pastor out of obedience to God, whether you think they deserve it or not, you honour him. Sometimes things may not be the way you would have wanted them to be but it is vital to understand that our pastors are the representatives of God here on earth as equal as our biological parents that we show and demonstrate high level of respect and value to.

Pastors are sent by the Almighty God to preserve lives in specific congregations or churches and we have the duty to bear them up in prayers, and lift them in high esteem.

It is necessary not to forget that they are also human beings and must be experiencing some form of difficulties or challenges in their personal life. So there is the need to remember them in prayers and to honour them accordingly. I have also discovered that to honour your pastors as an armour bearer is to be faithful to them irrespective of their shortcomings.

Being faithful to your pastors that you are under and serving as an armour bearer, you are opening yourself for greater and higher dimensions of supernatural blessings. There is no way one can be faithful to another without respecting them.

Another way to demonstrate your honour to your pastor is to respect them so highly above your personality.

Sometimes you need to spearhead some specific occasions, birthday, Father's Day and Mother's Day for them to honour them. It is said that October is the month for appreciation of pastors; so perhaps something special could be done in the month of October. This could be organised by you the armour bearers to honour your pastors.

Whenever you get close to your pastors (men/women of God), please do not see them after the flesh. Avoid being physically close to them because this will create an attitude of equality.

The word of God says that, "Know no man after the flesh" (2 Corinthians 5:16).

When we look at the life of Ham, he got too close to Noah (MAN OF GOD) and saw his nakedness. The mistake here was that he should have honoured the assignment, duty, office of Noah rather than the nakedness (behaviour, appearances, and looks). Here, we discovered that as an armour bearer, you may have the chance or privilege to get close to your pastors than any other church members. You need to respect that office and do not join other members to speak against them.

Honouring your pastors does not mean to judge them by their looks or speech. Regardless of these shortfalls, you need to honour them as God has commanded. You need to consider those who labour in word amongst you and count them worthy of double honour. For the years of serving my bishop (MICHAEL HUTTON-WOOD), I noticed that pastors offered themselves to be used fully by God and the Holy Spirit to feed the flock.

One thing I have also learnt over the years of being an armour bearer is that the job of being a pastor is not that easy and it is a job for life. Therefore, as an armour bearer, you are there to provide encouragement and support to your pastors to motivate them to carry on preaching the pure Word of God.

> "And we beseech you, brethren, to know them which labour among you, and are over you in the Lord, and admonish you; And to esteem them very highly in love for their work's sake. And be at peace among yourselves"

**1 Thessalonians 5:12-13, KJV**

You can honour your pastors by taking time out of your busy schedules to visit their homes and offices to assist them especially their partners (husband or wife) depending on the leader of the church. Sometimes you can go and wash dishes, clean up, tidy the sitting areas, store up some food stuffs left in the car overnight due to the pressure of the ministry.

This is to show them that you honour them and appreciate the great work they are doing in the Kingdom of God. This serves as a form of encouragement to them. It is also necessary to speak words of encouragement to them to reassure them that all is well with them and let them know that you are praying with them. I can assure you that when you begin to honour them this way, it will propel them to keep the fire going in their ministry. Honour your pastors.

## DUTY 4: RUN WITH YOUR PASTOR'S VISION

To run is to be in motion or to chase a course of action. Vision can be regarded as purpose or mission. Therefore it is possible to say that our pastors are vision carriers. They carry the vision (purpose, mission, agenda, and mandate) of God for every church. The question here is; how can you run with the vision of your pastors as an armour bearer?

We have established that pastors are the vision carriers and therefore as armour bearers, we need to develop the attitude to stand and run with those visions. The duty of an armour bearer is to keep your eyes fixed up exclusively on that dream or goal your pastors have by ensuring that nothing hinders them from achieving that purpose of God for the church. You will need to remain absolutely focused, disregarding any distractions wherever they may be coming from. You will require extreme devotion, commitment and the determination to make sure that your pastors achieve that vision on their lives.

I believe that every church has their own visions and mandate given to the leaders and it is our (ARMOUR BEARERS') sole responsibility to motivate them to fulfil the said visions and mandate. . You may be the one the pastor may call upon to talk or make some crucial decision regarding the direction of the church especially when it comes to church building, evangelism etc. You are there to provide support to them (pastors) when other leaders are thinking of going back or leaving the church due to misunderstanding. You are their backbone in that respect.

Sometimes your pastors may come up with an idea of a new project within the church premises. You as an armour bearer need to organise and motivate the members of the church to contribute and to provide when required and needed. Your duty as an armour bearer is to make sure that your pastors are not carrying the burden alone.

Many armour bearers cannot understand why they have to work on their pastor's vision or dream, rather than on their own vision. Most often some think that running or working on the pastor's vision means a neglect of their own dreams and callings. On the contrary, it is not so and not true.

It takes revelation of how God works for some armour bearers to truly and fully understand that when they serve another man's vision, they are indirectly serving their dreams and visions into fruition. That is the spirit and the sacrifices of a pastor's armour bearer.

Are you ready and prepared to lay down your life for God's vision and dream for your church through your pastor?

I have come across many so-called armour bearers who claim to love their pastors and their vision but are nowhere to be found simply because they are or were just interested in the glory of being called an armour bearer without thinking of going through the process of serving to the end.

They get offended and then leave their church without telling the pastor the reason for leaving. Some even go to extent of sending text messages to their pastors letting them know that they have moved on to pursue the calling of God upon them. Hence, they leave their positions vacant without anybody stepping in or training anybody to take their place.

Many so-called armour bearers cannot commit to service for the long haul in their pastor's life because they are internally afraid that if they do, they will not be able to accomplish their own calling and dream. So many connect without committing totally and never put their neck to the work of building the vision of the ministry.

> "Knowing that whatsoever good thing any man doeth, the same shall he receive of the Lord, whether he be bond or free"

**Ephesians 6:8 KJV**

I can testify that working on your pastor's dream and upholding the vision of the house sets God in motion to accomplish your dreams in your life. There is a double blessing when you become diligent and busy in serving your pastor. God becomes active in fulfilling the dreams of your house, your family, protection for your children, and many more.

Remember that until Joseph interpreted the dream of another person in the prison, his dream of being a leader and president was still with him without being recognised. That dream was hidden within him even though God had promised him and had shown him vision upon vision. Those dreams could not be acknowledged by the king. What does this mean to you? Before God would manifest his dreams, Joseph had to work on the dreams of others and become skilful at it.

Joseph laid down his life to serve or assist the butler and the baker while in prison; regardless of his own dream and vision. So God could not ignore him but to meet and show him favour in the presence of the king. This is because he was very faithful in serving others with the heart of loyalty to bring his dream out to change his destiny.

Always remember that if your PASTORS are happy, you will be happier and both of YOUR lives will reflect that.

> "Each of us had a dream the same night, and each dream had a meaning of its own. Now a young Hebrew was there with us, a servant of the captain of the guard. We told him our dreams, and he interpreted them for us, giving each man the interpretation of his dream. And things turned

out exactly as he interpreted them to us: I was restored to my position, and the other man was hanged"

**Genesis 41:11-13**

"And whatsoever ye do, do it heartily, as to the Lord, and not unto men"

**Colossians 3:23**

"And in every work that he began in the service of the house of God, and in the law, and in the commandments, to seek his God, he did it with all his heart, and prospered"

**Chronicles 31:21**

"Whatsoever thy hand findeth to do, do it with thy might; for there is no work, nor device, nor knowledge, nor wisdom, in the grave, whither thou goest"

**Ecclesiastes 9:10**

"And let us not be weary in well doing: for in due season we shall reap, if we faint not"

**Galatians 6:7-9**

Your promotion, protection, provision, and prolonged life is determined by serving and running with your pastors vision.

The way and manner you perceive your pastors will surely determine the way you see them, relate to them, speak with them, etc. It also determines what you expect from them. Let us bear in mind that our pastors are not just ordinary people in our lives. They are not our co-equal or football mates, classmates; but servants and the mouth of God.

Remember that they are called to preach, teach, feed, admonish and empower each member of the church to stand on the sure Word of God to fulfil their respective destinies and above all, to make it to heaven when the rapture takes place. Pastors are vessels, gifts, and destiny carriers. Therefore serving them enables you to catch their spirit. Pastors are the ones that God uses to change people's destinies through the Word of God that they preach. You gain wisdom and understanding as you serve and motivate them. You also catch the fire within them and sooner or later you will experience the supernatural move of God in your life.

As you serve as an armour bearer in your pastors' lives faithfully, your life will never be the same again. It will take on a new shape and form to the glory of God.

## DUTY 5: OBEY AND BE SUBMISSIVE TO YOUR PASTORS

> "Obey them that have the rule over you, and submit yourselves: for they watch for your souls, as they that must give account, that they may do it with joy, and not with grief: for that is unprofitable for you"

**Hebrews 13:17**

Your obedience to your pastors brings divine direction and profit to you and your generation.

I have observed the pain and hurts that pastors go through when those that they especially (armour bearers) have taught the pure Word and motivated to comply with the Word of God, disobey and do the very things they have told them not to do. That can be very painful. Some pastors get hurt so deeply to see their armour bearers disobey or ignore the counsel of God that they share into their lives.

Obeying your pastor means that you value their advice and not ignore what they give you. Don't make the mistake by trusting your own wisdom as well as your own heart.

The Word of God states that a "godly pastor shares precepts from God's Word because he desires not only to serve God but to feed spiritual food to the flock that will result in their experiencing the abundant life Jesus promised" (John 10:10b).

In most churches today it is said that most people are yearning for positions but are not ready and prepared to obey other church leadership above them. This makes it necessary that every armour bearer cultivates the spirit of obedience and submission to their pastors.

There will be many instances where other members will approach to break away from your church and form their own ministry. Some may even go the extent to lure you with money to come and join them to be the next or associate minister or pastor in their church.

As an armour bearer, you need to remain faithful and obedient to your leader (pastors) and never allow any body to deceive to you to break away from your leader. Never allow others to make you think that you are now equal with your pastors and let it not get into your head to rebel against authority.

Obeying your pastors gives credit to your sacrifice and service because the anointing you honour is the same that honours you.

As an armour bearer, when you start to disobey your pastors and begin to see yourself as your own person, the spirit of Lucifer, Miriam and Aaron, Dathan and Abiram, Korah, Achan, Absalom, Adonijah, Demas, Alexander the Coppersmith, Judas and Elymas set in to make you think that you can also be a king. You will begin to develop an attitude thinking that you can fly higher than your pastors. Watch it. You will not get far.

One thing disobedience does to a rebellious armour bearer is that it makes them think, rely and depend on themselves and think that God can also speak with them too. So they rebel against authority.

Disobedient armour bearers tend to abuse their position because they lack correction, direction and the leading of their pastors. Sometimes these individuals go about telling people that they are also appointed by God when in real life, they have broken away from their spiritual family tree (church) and are like the prodigal son using God's name to cover their rebelliousness.

As an armour bearer, your obedience and submission to your pastors indicate that you fear and respect God. You are not just obeying your pastors but you are also obeying God who has sent and given them command to watch over you.

> "Remember those who rule over you, who have spoken the word of God to you, whose faith follow, considering the outcome of their conduct"

**Acts 13:7**

You obey your pastors simply because you respect and see them as people who are more powerful in the (sight of God) than you are. This enables you to do your service unto the Lord with a peace and quiet spirit of heart. The Will of God not be done with a disobedient heart. Doing the Will of God involves seeking and then obeying God's Will through the pastors He has chosen for us to serve. Whatever you do as an armour bearer, do it with a joyful and respectful heart.

> "Obey those who rule over you, and be submissive, for they watch out for your souls, as those who must give account. Let them do so with joy and not with grief, for that would be unprofitable for you"

**Hebrews 13:17**

> "Remember those who rule over you, who have spoken the Word of God to you, whose faith follow, considering the outcome of their conduct"

**Hebrews 13:7**

> "I have posted watchmen on your walls, O Jerusalem; they will never be silent day or night. You, who call on the LORD, give yourselves no rest"

**Isaiah 62:6**

> "Son of man, I have made you a watchman for the house of Israel; so hear the word I speak and give them warning from me"

**Ezekiel 3:17**

> 66
> **"Submission to God-appointed leadership will always cause God's favour to flow in your life."**
> 
> **UNKNOWN AUTHOR**

# DUTY 6: SPEAK WELL OF YOUR PASTORS

"The good man brings good things out of the good stored up in his heart, and the evil man brings evil things out of the evil stored up in his heart. For out of the overflow of his heart his mouth speaks"

**Luke 6:45**

As an armour bearer, one of the greatest things you can do for your pastors is to speak well of them. This shows your loyalty and faithfulness to them. This is not to say that when they are wrong you should side with them but never speak against them publicly. Find the right time and moment to raise issues with them especially when you need to do so. First of all, go to God in prayer and pray that the Holy Ghost Himself will reveal things to them in the area that are needed most.

Never come to the point where you think your voice should be heard above your pastor's. Over the years of my services as an armour bearer, never once have I tried to point or speak against my bishop; because he is my head and nobody speaks evil against their head. Your pastors are the head of the ministry and the church. See them as such and do everything in your power to defend them and never join gangs to speak about them because other members are watching your attitude and conduct to judge you.

Ensure that whenever you open your mouth to speak about your pastors, you speak only encouraging words. People will only get to know your pastors very well because of the way you speak about them. I have always said to people that our pastors will be crucified or celebrated based on the word we speak about them either in public or in secret. The Lord God has commanded us not to touch His servant. "Do not point a finger at my anointed servant, do my prophet no harm," says the Lord of hosts.

> "And Miriam and Aaron spoke against Moses because of the Ethiopian woman whom he had married: for he had married an Ethiopian woman."

**Numbers 12:1**

You will notice here that anybody who speaks against men of God like your pastors does that at their own peril. Whatever you do not understand, get to your pastors and reason with them and ensure that you really understand the level at which they are coming from or stand. This makes it easier for you to relate well with them. It makes you develop the spirit of tolerance and patience for them always; especially when it comes to things outside the pulpit.

One other way of addressing your own discouragement is to motivate your pastors. Proverbs 11:25 says, "He who refreshes others will himself/herself be refreshed." Instead of looking for someone to pick you up, look around to see who you can pick up. Thank goodness, we can be motivators even when we feel discouraged and in the process of time you may become a motivator and lessen yours.

> "Not forsaking the assembling of ourselves together, as the manner of some is; but exhorting one another; and so much the more, as ye see the day approaching"

**Hebrews 10:25 KJV**

One good cure for discouragement is simply to get involved in church activities. For example; get involved in prayer meetings, soul winning, etc. Find a department within your church and be committed and loyal to, aside your duty as an armour bearing. This may encourage and change your moods.

At times when you are discouraged, you become frustrated, unmotivated and let down, but as you join forces with other believers to undertake God's work, you will become motivated and encouraged and, of course, uplifted, overcoming fear and anxiety.

Spend some time in the fellowship of those people with strong faith, share the Word of God together and meditate on it. You need to get together more often, even in the midst of your busy schedules, because you need one another to stay encouraged.

Encouragement is one of the most important things we all need and expect when we are discouraged or feeling down. That is why in Jude 1:19-21, the Bible says, "But you, beloved, building yourselves up on your most holy faith, praying in the Holy Spirit, keep yourselves in the love of God, looking for the mercy of our Lord Jesus Christ unto eternal life."

Your pastors need positive and productive people in their lives to motivate them to keep pressing on in the faith, to build them in the pastoral journey so that they do not lose hope but to stay on the course and stay alert. That is why you are there to be courageous and defensive. Joshua 1:6 commands you to be bold and courageous in your service. Galatians 6:1 educates us that, "Brethren, if a man is overtaken in any trespass, you who are spiritual restore such a one in a spirit of gentleness, considering yourself lest you also be tempted." This is to say that your pastors need your fellowship and encouragement to motivate them.

I have developed the habit of not joining individuals who set themselves apart to listen and partake in gossip especially about my bishop. Never engage in a group of people who speak against or listen to gossip or slander about your pastor. You are there to defend him; not to sell him to any committee within or outside the church. Any time you come across people speaking against your pastors, stop them immediately because you will be the next in line that they will be discussing. Always refuse any negative comments made against your pastors to prevent further spread of gossip.

> "Do not receive an accusation against an elder except from two or three witnesses."

**1 Timothy 5:19**

One of the greatest things that affects the attitude of some armour bearers is that they expect their pastors to be so perfect. Hey! They are humans too just like us all and therefore we need to relate with them with patience. The same pressure you go through is exactly as they are going through, even more than you are. Never speak against them. Speak well of them to motivate them to keep the fire burning in their spirit.

Pastors spend more time preparing and delivering the pure Word of God each week and therefore when we speak good things concerning them, it goes a long way to empower them to get better and better in their ministration. Discouragement and pressure of ministry will drop off their shoulders when they know that you are speaking well of them.

This makes it more interesting when you as an armour bearer take it upon yourself to know the full mission of your pastors and the church. You align yourself with your pastors and stand with the very goals they set and their values. Their priorities become your priorities, too. You become so dependable and reliable in the life of your pastors. Don't ever be the one criticising pastors and the leaders around. Yours is to work to ensure that souls are saved. Devout your time and energy to be a motivator in your pastors' lives by speaking well of them.

Serving as a pastor's armour bearer is a remarkable and awesome blessing and privilege. Be an asset, not a liability, in the lives of your pastors.

## DUTY 7: SUPPORT YOUR PASTORS FINANCIALLY

"Let the elders who rule well be counted worthy of double honour, especially those who labour in the Word and doctrine"

**1Timothy 5:17**

"This they did, sending their gift to the elders by Barnabas and Saul"

**Acts 11:30**

Another way to demonstrate your sincerity is by giving to your pastors. Most pastors have family commitment and other household responsibilities to cater for. Therefore, it is your duty as an armour bearer to support your pastors financially. Please note here that you give according to how the Lord has blessed you. It is very necessary that you get the understanding right. Nobody gives what they do not have. So I am not saying that you should steal to bring to your pastors especially when you are not receiving any financial income.

Remember the story of the widow of Zarephath who gave her last to the servant of God and her life was transformed. It is necessary to know that when we give or support our pastors financially, God Himself comes in to bless us in supernatural ways.

When you sow financial seeds/money in the lives of your pastors, it enables them to buy the things they needed most. A financial gift supports them to pay some basic bills that are outstanding and a burden to them that the ministry is not aware of. My family has taken it upon itself to buy our pastors their favourite brand of rice each month. Sometimes, when we get so busy and we miss any month, we ensure that we double the bags of rice to make up for the months that we missed. This has brought about some blessings and protection from God in the lives of our children, my spouse, and mine. Some go to the extent of washing their cars weekly to demonstrate their personal love to them. What can you do? What can you give? Start from where you are and work your way up when things get better for you. Not that they need it to survive. It is just a part of your duty as an armour bearer to sow financially into your pastors' lives.

> "The labourer is worthy of his wages...."

**1 Timothy 5:17-18**

Be committed to support your pastors in times of financial hardship. Be their friends who will actually understand them and extend your arms to them especially when they have little children. Amos 3:3 says that, "How can two walk together except they be agreed." As an armour bearer, you need to demonstrate your agreement to your pastors and know how they feel financially.

Never sow unwillingly and grudgingly into your pastor's life because it's not going to bear anything in your life.

> "So let each one give as he purposes in his heart, not grudgingly or of necessity; for God loves a cheerful giver."

**2 Corinthians 9:7**

We observed in the life of Paul that he had to explain to the Corinthian church that God would provide for their needs if they cultivate and develop the attitude of giving to (men of God/pastors) and also towards other members of the church. The Word of God cannot lie; what God has said in His Word is exactly what He will do.

The Word of God says that, "He who sows sparingly will also reap sparingly, and he who sows bountifully will also reap bountifully. So let each one give as he purposes in his heart, not grudgingly or of necessity; for God loves a cheerful giver. And God is able to make all grace abound toward you, that you, always having all sufficiency in all things, have abundance for every good work. As it is written: 'He has dispersed abroad, He has given to the poor; His righteousness remains forever.' Now may He who supplies seed to the sower, and bread for food, supply and multiply the seed you have sown and increase the fruits of your righteousness, while you are enriched in everything for all liberality, which causes thanksgiving through us to God" (2 Corinthians 9:6-11).

> "He who receives you receives me, and he who receives me receives Him who sent me. He who receives a prophet in the name of a prophet shall receive a prophet's reward; and he who receives a righteous man in the name of a righteous man shall receive a righteous man's reward. And whoever in the name of a disciple gives to one of these little ones even a cup of cold water to drink; truly I say to you, he shall not lose his reward"
>
> **Matthew 10:40-42**

## DUTY 8: BE COMMITTED TO SERVE YOUR PASTORS

I have come to accept that to be a pastor's armour bearer you need a greater dimension of commitment. This kind of commitment only comes to you when you ask for it through fervent prayer (James 1.5-6; Matthew 7:7). You need to be committed to serve because your pastors sometimes get very busy that the faint will not be able to stand. As an armour bearer, you need to establish a course of action that will help to achieve your pastors' goals (purpose) for the day. This comes through commitment to ensure that nothing side-tracks or distracts your pastors before service especially on Sunday mornings. It is your duty to ensure that everything that needs to be done before your pastors come is done.

> "Commitment is the enemy of resistance, for it is the serious promise to press on, to get up, no matter how many times you are knocked down."
>
> **DAVID MCNALLY**

To be commitment is to be totally sold out to your duties, works or assignments. No holding back due to ill-treatment. You are full persuaded and dedicated to your service just to bring honour to God and your pastors. According to my bishop, commitment can be likened to an analogy of chicken producing an egg, cow producing milk and pig providing sausages and bacon by dying to illustrate the high level of commitment. The price to pay as armour bearer demands that your life becomes like the pig to sacrifice and lay your life down for your pastors to see the Kingdom of God established in your church.

When you look at the lives of Noah, Abraham and Moses, they were committed to their assignment God gave them. They were sold out for service. No wonder their lives are examples for us to emulate.

> "Labour not for the meat which perisheth, but for that meat which endureth unto everlasting life, which the Son of man shall give unto you: for him hath God the Father sealed"
>
> **John 6:27**

It is evident that nothing significant and tremendous happens to you until you are totally sold out for service to your pastors.

Your dedication to God's servant will eventually determine how distinguished your life becomes among your peers. Esther was so dedicated and committed to her services that she vowed to die in the course of it (Esther 4:16).

Being an armour bearer, you need to understand that your pastors' spiritual warfare can be very draining and demanding and you are needed to be committed to it to see victory. Although others may think it's cool and nice to be a pastor's armour bearer, sometimes when the rubber hits the road, they will be expecting you to give in and back down. What they don't know is that it takes the brave to swim in the troubled waters through commitment to survive and to stand earnestly for the faith.

**Your commitment to the services of God and your pastors is what God uses to commission you into greatness.**

A story was told of David's mighty men (ARMOUR BEARERS) that one day, David was very thirsty and needed water to drink from Bethlehem. We were told that these individuals (ARMOUR BEARERS) took it upon themselves through commitment to get the water to their leaders (PASTORS). The story continues to narrate that David's men fought the enemies preventing them from getting the water to him through a heavy price which could have cost their personal lives. These men took the initiative to go out of their way to do this just to bring some water to their leader (2 Samuel 23:8-39).Commitment to the services of God and pastors is desperately needed in the life of anybody thinking of being a pastor's armour bearer and to be filled with the Holy Spirit to empower them to serve unreservedly.

The question is; how faithful and committed are you to get things done for your pastor without being told to do so?

Are you committed to stand by your pastors to defeat the enemies preventing the growth of your church?

What about those who gossip and speak evil against your pastors?

It will take a serious level of commitment, dedication and sacrifice to go the extent to lay your life DOWN for your pastors whom you are serving as an armour bearer.

"Commit thy way unto the Lord: trust also in Him; and He shall bring it to pass"

**Psalm 37:5**

# Chapter Two

◆

# CULTIVATING THE FRUIT OF THE SPIRIT

◆

"But the fruit of the Spirit is love, joy, peace, longsuffering, gentleness, goodness, faith, meekness, temperance: against such there is no law"

**Galatians 5:22-23**

"Behold my servant, whom I uphold; my elect, in whom my soul delights; I have put my spirit upon him: he shall bring forth justice to the Gentiles"

**Isaiah 42:1**

One of the areas in our lives as pastor's armour bearers that we need to cultivate and nurture is the fruit of the spirit. The fruit of the spirit is actually the fruit of the Holy Spirit within us. When we allow the Holy Spirit to work on us, cultivate and prune us, we begin to grow in the things of God like a tree that is cultivated and, later, bears fruits.

Every individual has some form of ego power in them which actually controls the way and manner that they react, behave, interact and serve in the house of God. That ego can be classified as a 'spirit' which then bears some form of fruit that people see when we are under pressure or happy.

The Holy Spirit also dwells within us so much so that it also produces fruit which is called the fruit of the spirit because it is a fruit of the Holy Spirit. This is the reason why as armour bearers, we need to ensure that we are full of the Holy Spirit daily so that we can be able to produce the fruit of the spirit to edify the Kingdom of God. This also helps you to humble yourself under your pastor to serve as unto the Lord. By cultivating the fruits of the Spirit you develop the spirit of meekness and many others that are the very attributes of the Holy Spirit.

To be an effective and loyal armour bearer to your pastors, you need to pray daily for the fruits of the spirit because when situations get challenging, it is the fruit of the Holy Spirit that set in to calm you down. It takes the fruits of the spirit to make you dependable, loyal, faithful, and steadfast to stand with your pastor. Without the Holy Spirit bearing fruits in your life, your services to God and His pastors will not be effective.

This can only be real in our lives when each and every one of us seeks to develop personal relationship with the Holy Spirit daily so as to follow His leading. I have personally experienced this myself that I am able to relate well, serve, and love my bishop because I commit myself more to be used by the Holy Spirit and subject to His leading in my life before I appear before him (bishop).

This has also made me to develop the spirit of discernment as to what to do at the right time, how to do things so as not to grieve the Holy Spirit and the spirit of my pastors. It is very crucial that we value the leading of the Holy Spirit in our services to pastors. The Holy Spirit is not the author of confusion so your life cannot be in confusion. He will lead you to operate orderly.

> "And grieve not the Holy Spirit of God, by whom you are sealed unto the day of redemption"

**Ephesians 4:30**

Any Spirit-filled armour bearer has the capacity and enablement to bear the fruits of the Spirit. Why? Because the Holy Spirit is very productive and will definitely produce its fruits in you. Consequently you need to put your flesh under the control of the Holy Spirit for it to be worked and cultivated. It's not going to be easy but with prayer and sincere desire for it, you will begin to bear the fruit of the spirit as an armour bearer.

How many of pastors' armour bearers are ready to be pruned, corrected, led, instructed and rebuked by the Holy Spirit?

Are you even filled with Holy Spirit?

Are you bearing the fruits of the Spirit?

Are you nurturing the fruits of the Spirit in you?

Is the evidence of the fruits of the Spirit showing in your services to God and your pastors?

"But you are not in the flesh, but in the Spirit, if so be that the Spirit of God dwell in you. Now if any man have not the Spirit of Christ, he is none of His"

**Romans 8:9**

---

## What are the fruits of the Spirit?

---

"But the fruit of the Spirit is love, joy, peace, longsuffering, gentleness, goodness, faith, meekness, temperance: against such there is no law"

**Galatians 5:22-23**

These are areas in which we (pastors' armour bearers) must be cultivating regularly to be able to stand for the Lord and His ministry (the church).

### THE SPIRIT OF LOVE

This is not limited to emotional feeling or mere words that we speak about. The spirit of love is the spirit of God's kind of love (AGAPE LOVE). The Word of God says categorically that, "Greater love has no man than this, that a man lay down his life for his friends" (John 15:13).

From this passage, our Lord and Saviour Jesus Christ was trying to demonstrate to us the meaning of LOVE. The God kind of love is to be committed to an individual to the point of death. This means laying down your life for somebody. We saw this in the life of David. We observed how his men laid their lives down to go and get him some water to drink irrespective of the danger they faced. If you say you love your pastor so much, are you prepared to sacrifice your life to protect, defend and promote the vision that God has given him/her without you feeling irritated?

Over the years of my service to my bishop, I have come to acknowledge that to be able to exercise or demonstrate the God-kind of love to others especially men and women of God, one needs to put the concern and vision of the church above one's chief source of joy.

In Philippians 2:3, we learnt that whatever we do to others or men of God should not be done in vainglory. *"Let nothing be done through strife or vainglory, but in lowliness of mind but let each other esteem others better than themselves."* Jesus Christ Himself made it clear in John 13:35, that, *"By this shall all men know that you are my disciples, if you have love one to another."*

I have realised that some people get frustrated whenever they feel unloved or unappreciated by others especially the pastors they are serving as armour bearer. The reason is that they depend on these individuals to make them happy and if they don't, then they crush and get upset. The fruit of love produced in you by the Holy Spirit will actually empower you to demonstrate and show love for others irrespective of how they treat you. Be willing to be the first to love others and they will love you back.

Your love-inputs to others determine others' output of love to you.

"Be not deceived; God is not mocked; for whatsoever a man soweth, that shall he also reap"

**Galatians 6:7**

One of the greatest benefits of sowing the seed of love is that you begin to reap in multiples. By that, people you do not know gravitate towards you because of the spirit of love in you. My prayer is that you will grow in the spirit of loving your pastors and their vision as an armour bearer in Jesus name!

## THE SPIRIT OF JOY

"The vine is dried up, and the fig tree languishes, the pomegranate tree, the palm tree also, and the apple tree, even all the trees of the field, are withered, because joy is withered away from the sons of men."

**Joel 1:1-2**

The fruit or the spirit of joy is another one of what the Holy Spirit produces in our lives. This kind of joy enables you to go all out for the services of God because it comes from within you. This makes it easier to demonstrate your Christian behaviours and attitude regardless of the challenges you face along the way. You do things with gladness of heart to your pastors and other members of the ministry without feeling hurt or belittled by their action or attitude.

This kind of joy produces some form of pride with you to push you to serve in the house of God without being commanded or told to do one thing or the other. Your thoughts and actions demonstrate the feeling of cheerfulness any time you see your pastors and you cheer them on with all enthusiasm to preach the Word of God. A joyful attitude or thanksgiving brings things your way even if you do not seem to qualify for them. It is my personal observation that when we lose our sense of gratitude, we can lose our peace and joy, for our God desires that we enjoy peace and joy at all times(Romans 8: 28).Until your joy is full, you cannot serve any man. That is why our Lord Jesus Christ said, "My joy might remain in you, and that your joy might be full" (John 15:11). Also in Hebrews 1:9, the Bible says, "You have loved righteousness, and hated iniquity; therefore God, even your God, has anointed you with the oil of *gladness* above your fellows."

As pastors' armour bearers, we are being watched daily and being judged according to what, when, where and how we do things. The things we do can only be valued in the sight of God and man when we do them with gladness of heart and humility. The joy of the services we render to our pastors can only determine whether we have overcome self and are faithful and loyal sons to God's servant (PASTORS) by making good use of our gifts and talents to promote the work that God has given our pastors.

The spirit of joy enables us to enjoy peaceful and great relationship with our Lord and Saviour Jesus Christ. This is then demonstrated to others that we come across daily in our Christian walk and motivates us see that our living, service, worship and sacrifices are about God's divine purpose for our lives and not our own.

I have discovered that having the fruit of the spirit of joy enables or makes me understand God's agenda for my pastors and myself. This produces godly confidence and patience in me to understand the way my pastors operate, move, preach, teach, and do the things that they do. It also helps me to develop the right attitude towards them because my spirit is calm and I endure hardness like a soldier making my personal and Christian life meaningful and effective especially my devotion to the things of God and communion with my heavenly Father.

> "But the fruit of the Spirit is love, joy, peace, longsuffering, kindness, goodness, faithfulness, gentleness, self-control. Against such there is no law."
>
> **Galatians 5:22-23**

From the above passage **as pastors' armour bearers, there is the need to examine the following questions as to how you are developing or growing in the spirit of joy and gladness;**

1. How do I demonstrate the spirit of joy in my Christian life?
2. What are the things to do to cultivate the spirit of gladness more in my service to the LORD and my PASTORS?
3. What are the very hindrances to the development and flow of the spirit of joy within me?
4. How can I operate fully in the spirit of joy when I am faced with challenges and still remain faithful and loyal to my pastors?

## THE SPIRIT OF PEACE

From experience, I have discovered that a peaceful atmosphere is what we all desire to have especially when it comes to the mind. We all desire to have a peaceful lifestyle, church members and workers around us all the time. Most of us would like to be able to feel peaceful and not to be disturbed by troublesome events especially in church services.

Most often we want to see our pastors operate in a peaceful and calm manner when we make mistake or do something that we are not supposed to have done. We expect our leaders or pastors to act without being hostile to us.

The spirit of peace is produced by the Holy Spirit working and living in us. We cannot have a peaceful life without the Holy Spirit. This is the reason why as a pastor's armour bearer, you need to pray that the very peace of God will continue to work within you so as to remain calm to serve God.

Sometimes when we lack the peace of God in us, we get offended easily at the members and even the pastors we are serving because of lack of understanding and lack of love for ourselves. It is very important that we pray effectively for the spirit of peace to manifest in our lives especially in the areas of serving others who are younger than us or less educated. I have begun to pray more for the spirit of peace to grow in me so as to maintain my personal peaceful relationship with God, man and with myself.

This is because maintaining the spirit of peace with God motivates and encourages me to depend on Him for my family's provisions and trusting Him regardless of delays that may occur along the way. It is also my fervent prayer to cultivate the spirit of peace so as to relate appropriately with my pastors, leaders, members, family, children and even those who do not regard me as important in the ministry and to avoid unnecessary strife. This will also help me to live at peace with myself by not living a lifestyle of guilt .The word of God says that, "FOLLOW PEACE WITH ALL MEN."

"Follow peace with all men, and holiness, without which no man shall see the Lord"

**Hebrews 12:14**

"Peace I leave with you, my peace I give unto you: not as the world giveth, give I unto you. Let not your heart be troubled, neither let it be afraid"

**John 14:27**

> "Peace comes from within. Do not seek it without."
> **UNKNOWN**

As pastor's armour bearers and for the fact that we are Christians, it is required of us to pursue and cultivate peaceful attitude at all times because we do not want our attitude to drive the souls (members) away from the church. It should be our prayer to be empowered to grow in the fruit of the spirit (PEACE) (Psalm 34:14).

## THE SPIRIT OF LONGSUFFERING

"And we know that all things work together for good to them that love God, to them who are the called according to his purpose"

**Roman 8:28**

The spirit of longsuffering is also one of the fruits of the spirit that we need to cultivate as pastors' armour bearers and function effectively without fainting. "But he that shall endure unto the end, the same shall be saved" (Matthew 24:13).

Longsuffering simply means to suffer long by going through the process of facing challenges of lives, and trials. This requires a strong determination to exercise patience at all times. It is said that through suffering for an extended period of time, you can develop patience in waiting for God to work things out in His own time and in His own way. "Because you have kept the Word of my patience, I also will keep you from the hour of temptation, which shall come upon all the world, to try them that dwell upon the earth" (Revelation 3:10).

According to Sonya Triggs-Wharton (Christian thought) on the fruit of the spirit of longsuffering, we learnt that to endure means to carry on no matter what is going on around us. I have learnt that longsuffering helps to shape and develop our true and godly character and prepares us for the challenges we face as pastors' armour bearers Challenges make us stronger to mature in the faith and be able to face whatever difficulties we are sure to face.

Sometimes as a pastor's armour bearer, you could come across different kinds of people in the church who irritate, aggravate and disregard your authority as the pastor's armour bearer. Sometimes, some members get easily irritated and want to see the pastor immediately after church and are angry with you because you have asked them to wait for a while. You need to remain calm and let the fruit of longsuffering have its perfect work in your life.

The spirit of long suffering that we cultivate as pastors' armour bearers enables us to put aside any form of ideas and decisions to run with the vision and decisions of the leader we follow. Sometimes church activities can get so busy that there are a lot of demand on you to make decisions and if you are not prepared to endure hardness as a soldier, you will make a snap decision that could have a great effect on your pastor's vision for that day.

However, I have discovered that it pays to exercise or demonstrate the fruit of longsuffering or patience in times like these to avoid making unnecessary decisions which you may regret later.

I do appreciate that not every one of us has the same growth rate in dealing with spiritual things pertaining to how to serve under a busy pastor. I have personally experienced these in my church whereby people want to serve in one capacity in the church but need time to grow and mature in things of God. Some are like babies demanding breast milk every minute. Others are like young adults who need constant reminder of their responsibilities. Each and every one of us is unique in the church as the body.

When we look at the anatomy of the developmental stage of our body, not all parts develop at the same rate; some parts take time to develop and mature.. Therefore it is vital and crucial that we allow the fruit of patience to have its perfect work in our lives so as to be able to run with the vision of our pastors.

Any armour bearer without the spirit of longsuffering can never carry the mantle of his or her pastor to the end.

One thing I have discovered in ministry as my pastor's armour bearer is that sometimes I appreciate the importance of listening just to maintain a good communication skills with my bishop. To be able to do that, I have had to be very patient to allow him to relay his message across to me and if I found it necessary to respond, I do that with caution and courtesy. I do not speak back immediately to prove a point no matter how important my response will be. This has helped me to build the fruit of patience within me and enabled me to serve faithfully and remain loyal to my bishop (DESTINY FATHER).

> "Therefore I endure all things for the elect's sakes, that they may also obtain the salvation which is in Christ Jesus with eternal glory."

**2 Timothy 2:10**

## THE SPIRIT OF GENTLENESS

"Blessed are the meek: for they shall inherit the earth"

**Matthew 5:5**

The spirit of gentleness demands that whatever we do as a pastor's armour bearer is done with care. With the spirit of gentleness, you are able to function effectively without strife in your heart. You deal with your pastors with humility of heart and with respect. This enables you to relate and deal with them in such a manner of understanding their needs before your needs (HOPEFULLY).

Any thing you do, you consider them first by being very sensitive to their feelings. You can never understand an individual fully unless you have developed the fruit of gentleness to accommodate them with their ways and mannerisms.

> "O Jerusalem, Jerusalem, you that kill the prophets, and stone them which are sent unto you, how often would I have gathered your children together, even as a **hen gathers her chickens under her wings**, and you would not!"
>
> **Matthew 23:37**

> "But we were **gentle** among you, even as a **nurse cherishes her children**"
>
> **1 Thessalonians 2:7**

Meekness of heart is what God admires and adores in every believer especially pastors' armour bearers. In 1 Timothy 2:9, Paul the apostle rated it as more than precious gold. In fact, it is through the spirit of meekness that we relate or connect to God through the Holy Spirit.

The Holy Spirit does not seek itself but empowers us to live in the meekness of God which is the true nature of God. Meekness of heart enables you to demonstrate the love of God; because God Himself is love. As an armour bearer, you cannot demonstrate the love, patience, kindness and humility without the fruit of gentleness (1 Corinthians 13:4-7).

> "For I say, through the grace given to me, to everyone who is among you, not to think of himself more highly than he ought to think, but to think soberly, as God has dealt to each one a measure of faith"
>
> **Romans 12:3**

"Do not be wise in your eyes."

**Proverbs 3:7 NIV**

Sometimes it is possible to take offence by your pastor's attitude and behaviour especially when you are older, more intelligent, and cleverer than your pastor. However, it will take the fruit of meekness to remain humble and not get bitter but to continue to serve faithfully.

A meek and gentle armour bearer (person) will not think of himself to be better than the pastor he or she is serving because the Holy Spirit through the gentleness of heart will shield you from being angry or resentful. It is important to continuously pray for the Will of God to be done in your pastors' lives although there may be times that they suffer public embarrassment and pain, they will remain gentle in spirit.

"With all lowliness and meekness, with longsuffering, for bearing one another in love"

**Ephesians 4:2**

## THE SPIRIT OF GOODNESS

"Wherefore also we pray always for you, that our God would count you worthy of this calling, and fulfil all the good pleasure of his goodness and the work of faith with power"

**2 Thessalonians 1:11**

"For the fruit of the Spirit is in all goodness and righteousness and truth"

**Ephesians 5:9**

From the Webster Dictionary, it is possible to define goodness as the "quality of excellence in virtue; kindness; benevolence". The fruit of the Spirit is likened to seed sowing that needs some time to grow. It is not produced instantly like making popcorn. It must be cultivated through a strong desire and fervent prayer before it can grow within you to produce its evidence in your life.

> "But I say unto you, love your enemies, bless them that curse you, do good to them that hate you, and pray for them which despitefully use you, and persecute you"
>
> **Matthew 5:44**

Many of us believe that there is the need to allow the fruit of goodness to cultivate in our daily lives but how many are prepared to pay the price to be fruitful? Everything we do as armour bearers demands that we bear the fruit of the spirit so as to fulfil the mandate of God in us. It is very important that you get rid of the seeds of envy, jealousy, lust, worry, or fear. This is because if you do not, it will bear the same fruit and affect your relationship with your pastors and ministry.

The spirit of goodness enables you to bear fruits of kindness which then reflect in your attitude and character toward others by helping other believers to experience God's forgiveness.

> "And as you would that men should do to you, do you also to them likewise. For if you love them which love you, what thank have you? For sinners also love those that love them. And if you do good to them which do good to you, what thank have you? For sinners also do even the same.

And if you lend to them of whom you hope to receive, what thank have you? For sinners also lend to sinners, to receive as much again. But love you your enemies, and do good, and lend, hoping for nothing again; and your reward shall be great, and you shall be the children of the Highest: for He is kind unto the unthankful and to the evil"

**Luke 6:31-35**

## THE SPIRIT OF FAITHFULNESS

Another fruit of the Spirit of God is faithfulness. Through faith, we can be assured that God will not require us to endure more than we can bear.

"If thou faint in the day of adversity, thy strength is small"

**Proverbs 24:10**

"Without faith, it is impossible to please God"

**Hebrews 11:6**

The question that may be going through your mind right now could be; is it possible for an armour bearer to be attacked by satanic agents? The answer is yes. However, it does not make any difference because you are more than a champion.

Our faith in the Lord is tested daily and it takes the faithful ones to overcome. In 1 John 4:4, the Word of God encourages us that, *"Ye are of God, little children, and have overcome them: because greater is He that is in you than he that is in the world."*

It is not the time to quit or run away from your pastors when those evil days befall you or the ministry because it is your faith that is being tested and tried. You need to remain unwavering and resilient in the face of adversity. You cannot do that without the Spirit bearing fruit of faithfulness in your life.

The fruit of faithfulness provides strength in your life to be able to combat the ploy and of satanic works against you. As an armour bearer, you are not exempted from the attacks and ploys of the evil ones because you are the one who stands in the gap for your ministry and your pastors' vision for the church. The evil sees you as a threat against their works so they will do everything to frustrate your stand for the Lord and your pastors.

The fruit of faithfulness enables you to act on God's Word by trusting, hoping and believing in the goodness, and trustworthiness of God. In order to nurture the fruit of the spirit of faith, there is the need to read the Word of God concerning you. Faith comes by hearing, and hearing by the Word of God. It's the Word of God you hear that activates your joy inside you. This gets you to hold on to God's sure promises for your destiny. This is to say that faith in God's Word produces inner joy.

> "These things have I spoken unto you, that my joy might remain in you, and that your joy might be full"

**John15:11**

> "My brethren, count it all joy when ye fall into divers temptation; knowing this, that the trying of your faith worketh patience"

**James 1:2-3**

However, faith is nothing unless we live it; "And without faith it is impossible to please God" (Hebrews 11:6).

So no matter what you are going through in life as a pastor's armour bearer, the word of God encourages you to count it all joy because joy is the driving force to victory in Jesus name. Adversity will come but it is only those who have maintained their joy; enjoys the victory. Your circumstances may be showing negatives but remember that God has not left you or forsaken you. It is through your attitude and the steps of faith you take in God's word against those attacks of the enemies of your faith that will empower you to overcome and have a fruitful future.

> "I pray that out of His glorious riches He may strengthen you with power through His Spirit in your inner being, so that Christ may dwell in your hearts through faith"
>
> **Ephesians 3:16-17**

## THE SPIRIT OF MEEKNESS

> "Now the man Moses was very *meek*, above all the men which were upon the face of the earth"
>
> **Numbers 12:3**

The spirit of meekness is demonstrated in your humility and your good character. Being meek does not mean that you are stupid or foolish. Some may regard your meekness of heart as somebody to push over.

Hence, bearing the fruit of meekness does not mean that you are powerless to defend yourself but rather you hand everything to the power of the Holy Ghost to take control. In fact, it is the attitude of maintaining your good character in approaching God and your pastors through humility, realising that you can do *nothing* apart from God and your pastors' covering and leadership.

Most often you come across some individuals who allow the meekness or humility to be influenced negatively by others' bad behaviours. Yes, sometimes some people may think you are the foolish one for allowing your pastor to rebuke you openly without any reason. The spirit of meekness empowers you to keep your good character, being nice and humble even in the midst of difficult moments, and will make you to respond in love, harmony and unity.

## THE SPIRIT OF TEMPERANCE

"There has no temptation taken you but such as is *common to man*: but God is faithful, who will not suffer you to be tempted above that you are able; but will with the temptation also make a way to escape, that you may be able to bear it"

**1 Corinthians 10:13**

Temperance is another fruit of the spirit you need to cultivate as a pastor's armour bearer. It is one of the most important fruits you cannot have because it reveals your character and behaviour. You may have been gifted in the area of singing, teaching, preaching, serving and praying but if your character is not good; it will tarnish the gifts and talents that you have.

Character is everything you do especially in times of pressure from ministry and other things you may have. The spirit of temperance actually enables you to develop what is called, SELF-CONTROL.

## The ability to master or control one's self desire and passion

Your ability to control your character and self-desires is what makes others to trust and believe in you. It makes you very trustworthy. According to Eastwood Anaba, it is very "dangerous to put your trust in anybody who lacks self-control". It is the spirit of temperance that gives you the ability to retain and shape your character. It empowers you to extend love to your pastors and the members.

Without the spirit of temperance or self-control, you will not be able to control your emotions. It very important to know that when we allow the fruit of temperance to work in us, it becomes a precious tool in our lives to combat the plans of the enemies against our destiny..

## Eight Benefits of the Fruit of Temperance in an Armour Bearer's Life

1. The fruit of temperance prevents you from destroying yourself through compulsive attitude or behaviour.
2. Your life is more organised and planned.
3. It eradicates all forms of self-pity, feelings of a heavy heart, and produces a peace of mind in all that you set before you to achieve.

4. Your faith is increased and your hope is in the Lord; not man.

5. Your self-esteem and confidence are strengthened and you are motivated to keep the joy of the Lord burning within you.

6. You begin to act on the leadings of the Holy Ghost regarding the next level of your life and your family by making you very responsible in your approach.

7. The fruit of temperance enables you to focus on the Word of God and overcome temptations.

8. The fruit of temperance promotes and improves your relationships by cultivating patience and endurance in you.

"Those who do have God's Spirit dwelling in their minds should be exercising control over their emotions and actions, not 'giving place to the devil'"

**Ephesians 4:27**

The relationship between pastor and armour bearer should always be based on the fruit of the spirit to enable both of them to grow in the things of God to promote the agenda and the vision of God to meet the physical and spiritual needs of God's people.

# Chapter Three

◆

# INDEPENDENT SPIRIT: AVOID IT AT ALL COST

◆

"Now as touching things offered unto idols, we know that we all have knowledge. Knowledge puffeth up, but charity edifieth. And if any man think that he knoweth anything, he knoweth nothing yet as he ought to know"

**1 Corinthian 8:1-2**

Independent spirit is one of the major areas you need to fight against and consciously avoid in your life if you have to remain and maintain the right attitude as an armour bearer to your pastors. Most often this comes in when one becomes proud and begins to isolate themselves from the rest of the members. This type of spirit will only bring you down and cost you from receiving the blessing of your services unto the Lord.

Anybody who operates with an independent spirit causes havoc to the ministry and the God's vision. They cause disorder in the camp and rebel against authority and leadership. Independent spirit always wants to cause commotion and do not see to make peace. It also demonstrates the habit of pride. Such people are not ready to accept their faults and are quick to point fingers at others to prove a point that they are better and wise.

> "The fear of the Lord is the beginning of knowledge: but fools despise wisdom and instruction"

**Proverbs 1:7**

When you observe the Bible carefully, nothing positive is said about the spirit of independence. This is the main reason why as an armour bearer, you avoid that spirit in your life at all cost because it has the potential to bring you down.

> "For the day of the Lord of hosts shall be upon every one that is proud and lofty, and upon every one that is lifted up; and he shall be brought low"

**Isaiah 2:12**

It is very dangerous to operate with the independent spirit because it is sinful and deadly. Independent spirit sets in when you try to do things outside the plans and purpose of laid down rules to please yourself rather than God or the pastor you are serving. Independent spirit always gives an individual some false belief of thinking that they know everything under the sun.

> "He is proud, knowing nothing, but doting about questions and strifes of words, whereof cometh envy, strife, railings, evil surmising"

**1 Timothy 6:4**

When you begin to see yourself as God or greater than God's servant, your pastor, then the independent spirit is preying itself into your heart. This will eventually deceive you to believe that you are as great as your pastors and can operate better than them. Independent spirit is Satan's tool in luring you to fall from grace to grass. Lucifer operated in this spirit and that cost him his destiny and glorious future. He was kicked out from heaven because he was trying to operate independently.

> "How you are fallen from heaven, O Lucifer, son of the morning! How you are cut down to the ground, you who weakened the nations! For you have said in your heart: I will ascend into heaven, I will exalt my throne above the stars of God; I will also sit on the mount of the congregation on the farthest sides of the north; I will ascend above the heights of the clouds, I will be like the Most High"

**Isaiah 14:12-14**

Satan's main aim is to distract you from fulfilling God's divine mandate for your life. He will do everything possible to defocus you to ensure that your mind is taken off God and His servants (PASTORS). This will eventually make you think that you can do all things by your little mind and strength. As an armour bearer, you cannot operate in the flesh and in the spirit of God simultaneously. The devil's agenda is to make you fall from the divine protection, provision, and favour of God that he lost.

## Pride is the fruit of independent spirit

"For the day of the LORD of hosts shall be upon every one that is proud and lofty, and upon every one that is lifted up; and he shall be brought low"

**Isaiah 2:12**

From the above Bible verse, we learn that as a pastor's armour bearer, there is the tendency to become proud. However, you have the power to avoid any sign of pride in you. When you allow an independent spirit to take resident in your heart, you are trying to equate yourself with the pastor you are serving and deception will set in to destroy your destiny. *"Before destruction the heart of man is haughty, and before honour is humility (Proverbs 18:12).* Avoid it at all cost.

I have no doubt in my mind that King David acknowledged that he was likely to develop an independent spirit. So he prayed and asked the Almighty God to wash him from any form of pride and to cleanse his heart from unrighteousness and renew his spirit daily in His Word so as to keep his heart pure and free from independent spirits.

"Create in me a clean heart, O God; and renew a right spirit within me"

**Psalm 51:10**

## Humility is Your Highway to Greatness in Life

Most often some people tend to allow the negative ideas of others to influence their good character. It does not matter what people do to you; just maintain your good spirit and remain humble before your God and keep serving your pastors. Do not allow pride to set in because somebody elsewhere rated you so highly and promised to make you an assistant or resident pastor. These are the very traps that the devil will deplore to destroy your destiny.

Do not be wise in your own eyes because it will affect the flow of God's blessing to you and your family. One of the ways you can avoid independent spirit is to be vigilant of the devices of the enemies and humble yourself. It is possible to say that an independent spirit is the opposite of a humble spirit. Desire and develop the attitude to remain humble at all times in order to walk with God and to enjoy the full benefits of serving your pastors.

## Chapter Four

# HAVE A PURPOSE IN LIFE AS AN ARMOR-BEARER

As a pastor's armour bearer, it is very necessary that you acknowledge and appreciate your purpose in the life of your pastor. God is the Creator of life and He has a purpose for everything He created. God sent you to that church, or ministry to be a blessing to the pastor through your service. When you read Exodus 17:8-13, you will discover that a time came in the life of the children of Israel that they were attacked by their enemy (the children of Amalek) on their way to the Promised Land. It was a difficult moment for their leader, Moses, who needed the input of his leaders/ armour bearers in the leadership of Joshua.

Moses had to go to the mountain top to seek God's face for the direction he should take. So therefore, Aaron and Hur had to pray with Moses.

The Bible said that anytime Moses' hands were lifted up, victory came to the whole children of Israel but as soon as his hand came down, the children of Amalek were winning the battle. It was when Aaron and Hur discovered their purpose in the life of the Moses leader) to support Moses by holding his hands up to maintain the winning attitude of the whole camp of Israelite.

Conclusively, victories came to them all because the armour bearers (Joshua, Aaron and Hur) knew their purpose and took the opportunity to support their pastor/leader.

> "'For I know the plans I have for you,' declares the Lord, 'plans to prosper you and not to harm you, plans to give you hope and a future'"
>
> **Jeremiah 29:11**

God always wants a relationship with you. He wants a family relationship as He is our Father. God has a purpose and a plan for our lives. We learn from Hebrew 10: 7 that we are created for a specific purpose and as we identify that purpose and plan for our lives, we will begin to have a meaningful and successful life.

However, there is a need to have a plan by actually sitting ourselves down and undertake careful assessments of our needs and count the cost involved in the pursuit of our dreams.

Having a dream, plan and vision alone is not enough; the counting the cost of what it may take to realise the dream, plan, and visions is even more crucial. "For which of you willing to build a tower, doth not first, having sat down, count the expense, whether he has the things for completing" (Young's Literal Translation).

"Daniel purposed in his heart that he would not defile himself with the portion of the king's meat nor with the wine which he drank, therefore he requested the prince of the eunuchs that he might not defile himself"

**Daniel 1: 8**

Having a dream or a goal demands that you keep your eyes fixed exclusively on the dream or goal. You will need absolute focus, disregarding any distraction wherever they may be coming from. You will require extreme devotion, commitment and the determination to realise the dream or goal at all cost. Can you imagine what can happen when a footballer who has placed the ball at the spot kick and waiting for the referee to whistle for him/her take a penalty, decides to look aside whilst taking the penalty spot kick? Or the driver whilst reversing in the corner fixing his/her attention or eyes on the sandwich box by his side rather than concentrating on looking back and ensure safe driving?

A purposeful person is the one who defies all odds and stands by the truth. He may buy the truth but cannot sell it out. He/she is that individual who makes up his/her mind with its focus without allowing any wind of change to distract them. The ability to succeed in any endeavour of life and develop the capacity to impact positively on others is dependent on self-denials, sacrifices and commitments as evidenced in what we have read previously in the book of Daniel.

Clearly, Daniel's purpose was not to defile himself with the king's meat as he knew what the consequences could be. He no doubt denied himself so as not to conform to Babylonian custom.

Importantly, there is the need to have focus; a focus on the goal(s) of our dreams. The journey could be rugged; the tree full of thorns; disappointments and varieties of challenges; but you must not despair and lose the plot. Rather, hold firm and strong with a great faith like that of the proverbial mustard seed and remain focused on your dream, your goal and soon victory will be in sight in God's own time.

As we read in 2 Corinthians 4:18, "While we look not at the things which are seen but at the things which are not seen for the things which are seen are temporal, but the things which are not seen are eternal." When you are not moved or perturbed by the distractions, challenges and discouragements of loved ones and the devil's tricks in aborting your dream by taking your eyes off your target, in the process of time you will appreciate that these hold-ups are nothing compared to the fulfilment of a dream come true.

As we make up our minds to be in fellowship with our heavenly Father, and accepting His beloved Son Jesus Christ as our personal Saviour, who died on the cross that we may be saved, holding on to His promises through His Word, nothing, and l mean nothing should separate us from this relationship.

Be encouraged in the Lord as Daniel. In Habakkuk 2: 1-3, we read, *"I will stand upon my watch and set me upon the tower, and will watch to see what he will say unto me, and what I shall answer when I am reproved. And the Lord answered me, and said, write the vision and make it plain upon tables that he may run that readeth it. For the vision is yet for an appointed time, but at the end it shall speak and not lie, though it tarry, wait for it, because it will surely come, it will not tarry."*

There is the need to watch and pray concerning your purpose, goal or dream, and ensuring that your spirit man is driven daily as there is the tendency to lose focus. Protect and guard your purpose because it may not be so many people out there who may be happy about the fulfilment of your dream of achieving the grades at the university, winning that new contract for your business, or finding the dream of a life partner and the impending marriage, buying that new car or new home, given the truth of the presence of some pharaohs in our midst at this time who are desperate to kill that baby of a dream.

Joseph's account as recorded in biblical history as a dreamer and the events that unfolded into his being sold into slavery by his brothers, defying Potiphar, interpreting Pharaoh's dreams and finally becoming a prime minister in Egypt. This is undoubtedly the clearest testimony of the need to protect and guard our dreams.

You may have a dream about your future. Please share it only with your spiritual father, your heavenly Father's appointed representative, who will pray with you, encourage you and stand with you to see that dream come to pass in Jesus' name, Amen.

Nevertheless, should you for any other reasons share your dreams with people around you for which you may seem to be suffering today, do not be discouraged Do not throw in the towel. Keep the faith in our God; for in Him we trust

> **"Life without a purpose is life without meaning; and the greatest tragedy in life is not death, but life without purpose."**
> 
> **DR. MYLES MUNROE**

that hope abounds. He alone is your shield and buckler, and your protector who will stand with you and defend your course at all times. He will, in the process of time, definitely manifest His presence in your life, bringing victory to your door step.

> "Trust in the Lord with all thine heart; and lean not unto thine own understanding. In all thy ways acknowledge Him, and He shall direct thy paths"

**Proverbs 3:5-6**

In pursuit of one's purpose or dream, it is important that you identify your personal strength and weaknesses. This is the surest way of discovering the necessary steps needed to take to achieve your dream. There is no chance of realising a dream when we fail to plan and identify the processes involved in reaching whatever that dream may be.

Many people have failed in life not necessarily due to any interference or limitations of a kind imposed on them by any perceived circumstances or the enemy, but clearly due to their own lack of relevant and appropriate knowledge; which of course, is the power to success.

> "My people are destroyed for the lack of knowledge, because thou hast rejected knowledge"

**Hosea 4:6**

> "Give me now wisdom and knowledge that I may go out and come in before this people, for who can judge this thy people that is so great?"

**2 Chronicles: 1-10**

Solomon needed knowledge in pursing his vision, goal and purpose in life as a king. He knew that without knowledge and a discerning heart to govern God's people, he would not be able to distinguish between right from wrong (Isaiah 40:2).

My bishop once said that, "The future is secured by those who know how to sharpen and use their gifts, and their strength by identifying and making the most of the given opportunities." Patiently waiting on the Lord is necessary. It is equally important that we rely on informed knowledge to initiate the steps necessary to achieve the heights of life.

> "Your value of knowledge determines your upliftment in life."
> **PASTOR DAVID OYEDEPO JNR.**

Decisiveness of purpose is characterised by firmness and determination to achieve a dream or goal. However, as believers we need to appreciate and understand that decisiveness does not mean being stubborn, arrogant or hasty. It means being able to decide with speed and clarity of purpose in all matters.

Ruth, in her journey with her mother in-law, made a conscious and determined mind to follow her regardless of any price she may have to pay. Her determination, conviction, faith, commitment, humility, love, trust, self-belief and above all self-confidence as regards her purpose or goals are in no doubt worthy of emulation.

"And Ruth said, entreat me not to leave thee, or to return from following after thee, for whither thou goest, I will go; and where lodgest, I will lodge; thy people shall be my people and thy God my God. Where thou diest, will I die and there will I be buried, the Lord do so to me, and more also if ought but death part thee and me"

**Ruth 1: 16-17; Psalm 12: 7-8**

Samuel also was another personality that the biblical accounts indicated his courage, faith, and conviction to remain steadfast in achieving life's purpose. (1 Samuel 2: 26). So also was Jeremiah who stood firm in faith in his purpose of preaching the Word of God in the midst of his personal tribulations and trials. He nonetheless remained focused.

The moral lesson is the stark reminder for children of God to develop the capacity for endurance, patience, self-sacrifice and focus; which as demonstrated by these personalities are very crucial if we are to achieve the dreams and the plans that God has for us. For "Without a decision, no progress can be made." The Word of God cannot lie. Whatever He has promised concerning your destiny, He will fulfil and cause it to come to pass in your life. In every believer's hands there lie the seeds of failure or success.

Your decision regarding your purpose will only be achieved depending on your personal decisiveness of that sure purpose. Be decisive and let focus be your stock in trade, and as I always say, be like a postage stamp on a letter to your destination.

It is my personal appreciation that success is by choice; just as failure is. All great and successful persons make some choices at one time or the other; a choice which either promotes or collapses their business or enterprise.

In the pursuit of our individual dreams, there will be the occasion to make choices and the type of choices we make will determine our success or failure. We therefore need to be resolute and focused on our individual goals in order to make the best of all opportunities and choices available to us to fulfil God's agenda for us. Until we become obsessed with our purpose of life, we cannot be successful (Joshua 1:8). For it is when all our attention, time, and total efforts are given to our dreams, goals and visions that we can experience God's undeserved favour for our life and ministry.

Intimidation and bullying can be some of the methods or strategies that the enemy may employ to distract us from focusing on our purposes of life. Let us be like the three Hebrew men – Shadrach, Meshach and Abednego who, as we have already encountered in an earlier page, made determined choices and remained focused on their choices of serving only the true and living God, regardless of their experiences of the intimidation, with its prospects of defiling the Almighty God.

# Chapter Five

## DON'T ENTERTAIN DISCOURAGERS AROUND YOUR MINISTRY

"Now I beseech you, brethren, mark them which cause divisions and offences contrary to the doctrine which ye have learned; and avoid them. For they that are such serve not our Lord Jesus Christ, but their own belly; and by good words and fair speeches deceive the hearts of the simple"

**Romans 16:17-18**

Not entertaining discouragers is to avoid, turn away from, or even turn aside from those who cause offences and occasions of stumbling, turning away from dream killers, division makers and those who deliberately cause pain and havoc to your destiny.

It means that we are to stay out of their way and not fall in with them. Avoid them and have nothing to do with them. When it comes to your purpose in life, you need to actually search for those people who may discourage you from your assignment in life and avoid them completely.

"A righteous person is cautious with friendship, but the way of the wicked leads them astray"

**Proverbs 12: 26**

It is sometimes said that our countenance is always determined by the people we call loved ones and friends. They either add to us or subtract from us, making us or breaking us into such pieces beyond repairs. No doubt that people of wisdom are very careful about the type of people they associate with. No association leaves us neutral.

In Psalm 1:1, we are admonished not to even walk with them. We read, *"Blessed is the man that walketh not in the counsel of the ungodly, nor standeth in the way of sinners, nor sitteth in the seat of the scornful."*

In the pursuit of your individual plans and purposes in ministry, it is necessary that you do not entertain discouragers around you. Strive to avoid the company of those people who do not in any way share your vision or have your interest at heart.

> "People in our lives are like buttons in an elevator which take us up to the top floor, keep us on the ground or to the basement."
>
> BISHOP MICHAEL HUTTON- WOOD

Many a time, others in our lives may try discouraging us if we allow them Thus we must heed the advice to learn to listen to

God and let his Word dwell in us richly; making the conscious effort and decision in ignoring discouragers by avoiding them as much as possible as they are never part of God's promises to us.

> "My son, do not go along with them, do not set foot on their paths"

**Proverbs 1:15**

God has a purpose and plan for you; a bright and great future and you must not allow negative people to sow seeds of discouragement in your life and distract you from God's divine purpose for your life.

> "Oh, the joys of those who do not follow the advice of the wicked, or stand around with sinners, or join in with mockers"

**Psalm1:1**

Do not be discouraged by either the action or reaction of other people. Rather, use their actions towards you to develop and build a mind-set of progress and prosperity. Sometimes, you may come face-to-face with challenges and attacks, but remember the Word of God encourages us to be unmovable and unshakeable on these occasions.

We are empowered by God's purpose and plans for our lives, as his Word is always true and it will come to pass. Be consoled that no successful and forward-moving person goes through life without occasional episodes of discouragement. What is relevant and important is the development of appropriate attitude to the problem so as to withstand and overcome it.

This way, only one thing is certain - victory in the name of the Almighty God. Strangely, sometimes following this divine victory, the enemy may become jealous and envious of God's manifestation of His presence in your life. You may be discouraged because of unfulfilled desires and dreams of your life. You may have a desire for marriage, but the right man has not shown up all these while. Like Hannah, you may have had a dream of having a child; or passing your exams as a student, etc. These can present discouraging circumstances as was with Naomi and her calamities of lack of financial resources and the loss of her husband and her two sons (Ruth 1: 20-21).

As a pastor's armour bearer, you may be going through some financial difficulties which is causing great pain, anxiety and discouragement to your family; but never give up. Remember that your life is a seed in your pastor's life and God will cause it to turn things to your favour in Jesus' name.

Mary and Martha's experiences of discouragement we are told was out of the feeling of disappointment from the Lord Jesus our Saviour over the death of their brother, Lazarus. "If you had been here, my brother would not have died" (John 11:21). Peter experienced discouragement because of his personal failure. Having denied the Lord three times, he went out and wept rather bitterly; perhaps because he felt he had blown it big time. The concept of the rule of law dictates that 'Nobody is above the law'. Our Lord Jesus Christ Himself faced discouragement when the people at the time failed Him due to ignorance and lack of understanding during His ministry.

"These things I have spoken unto you, that in me ye might have peace. In the world ye shall have tribulation, but be of good cheer; I have overcome the world"

**John 16:33**

God understands discouragement; discouragement is a normal and unavoidable emotion that we must all deal with. It comes to us in different ways, for different reasons, and at different times, but rest assured that the grace of God is sufficient for us in our times of discouragement and He will surely see us through when we faint not as armour bearers.

"And He said unto me, my grace is sufficient for thee: for my strength is made perfect in weakness. Most gladly therefore will I rather glory in my infirmities, that the power of Christ may rest upon me"

**2 Corinthians 12:9**

## Chapter Six

♦

# FREE YOUR MIND FROM NEGATIVE THOUGHTS

♦

"For from within, out of the heart of men, proceed evil thoughts, adulteries, fornications, murders, thefts, covetousness, wickedness, deceit, lasciviousness, an evil eye, blasphemy, pride, foolishness: All these evil things come from within, and defile the man"

**Mark 7:21-23 KJV**

As an armour bearer, it is very necessary that you do not allow negative thoughts in your life or mind. Negative thoughts give an individual some wrong impression or false perceptions about themselves. This becomes a limitation or blockage of the true identity of your God-given talents and abilities. Negative thoughts affect how far you can go in ministry as an armour bearer.

This is why it is very vital that you invest yourself in prayer to avoid the negative thought coming to your mind. You need to identify the source of those thoughts and challenge them as they rear their ugly head in your mind. Discovery brings recovery. So in this case once you are able to discover the source of the negative thoughts and aware of the signs, you ask God for the empowerment to deal with them immediately before they destroy you.

> "I beseech you therefore, brethren, by the mercies of God, that ye present your bodies a living sacrifice, holy, acceptable unto God, which is your reasonable service. And be not conformed to this world: but be ye transformed by the renewing of your mind, that ye may prove what is that good, and acceptable, and perfect, will of God"
>
> **Romans 12:1-2**

Always renew your thoughts with the Word of God and use it to replace any form of negative thoughts that may arise.

As your pastor's armour bearer and the fact that you are a Christian, it is necessary to always check what goes on in your mind daily. I have come to notice that when we allow negative thoughts to stay in our mind, they create false perceptions of ourselves and later destroy the good relationship and good intentions we have about our pastors. They hinders our natural God-given talents and abilities to serve in God's house and his servant.

One of the devil's weapons against us as pastor's armour bearers is that he will use our thoughts to destroy us and once we are able to take control over these thoughts, we are en-graced and empowered to pull down every negative thought that could be building up in our minds.

"Repent therefore of this your wickedness, and pray God, if perhaps the thought of your heart may be forgiven you"

**Acts 8:22**

I would like to encourage you that anytime negative thoughts arise, engage in the Word of God to replace those thoughts. Our thoughts influence our existence, as well as our environment. Your happiness or unhappiness depends on whether your thoughts are ignited positively or negatively.

Romans 12:2 says, "Be not conformed to this world but be transformed by the renewing of your mind."

The word, "conform", means to assume an outward expression that does not come from an inward being. In other words, when you conform to something, you feel so much influenced that you begin to change the way you act. When you begin to conform to this world's system, you are not being faithful to who you really are on the inside. Behind the world's system, there is the evil one.

"Transform" means to assume an outward expression that comes from the inward being. This transformation needs to take place in our minds. The Bible cautions us that the carnal mind in itself is enmity against God. The transformation comes from the Word of God.

When you get the Word of God out of the pages of your Bible, read it and ponder over it, it gets into your mind and goes down into your spirit. When you keep doing this, you can see your mind lining up to your spirit. This is the key. Otherwise, there is this constant battle that goes on between your mind and your spirit.

You need to bear in mind that we are all eternal beings. We have an eternal spirit, we live in a mortal body and we have a soul that is made up of mind, will and emotions. The only doorway for the enemy into your soul is through your mind. Everything starts with a thought. Before you attempt to do anything, you think about it first. Your mind is the doorway to your deeds.

Be very careful about what you allow to control your mind which you think about. What you think about surely becomes your character and identity. The only way to be changed is by surrendering yourself and all ungodly thoughts to the Lord. How do you do this? **"By casting down imaginations, and every high thing that exalts itself against the knowledge of God, and bringing into captivity every thought to the obedience of Christ"** (2 Corinthians 10:5).

Although, sometimes negative thoughts pass through our mind, it is beneficial to combat it with the Word of God and to renew it daily with prayers. If you do not renew your mind daily with the Word of God, it will affect how you react around your pastors and other young believers. It is also affect your mood and behaviour.

One of the things I have done in the past especially when negative thoughts come into my mind (NOTE THAT I AM ALSO A HUMAN BEING), I disconnect myself from those individuals who take delight in speaking negative things about my pastor. Personally, I try to redirect my focus on how good my pastor (bishop) has been to me and my family during difficult times, how he paid off my car insurance, road tax, even gave me money to buy another car when the car I was using then got involved in an accident. How my bishop believed, trusted and relied on me as a faithful armour bearer for many years. This immediately flushed out any negative thoughts going through my mind.

> "And let the peace of God rule in your hearts, to which also you were called in one body; and be thankful"

**Colossians 3:15**

May I take this opportunity to empower and motivate you to stand on the sure Word of God and continuously develop intimacy with God to seek for strength and ability to free your mind from negative thoughts as they arise. The Word of God also encourages us that "…those who trust in the LORD will find new strength. They will soar high on wings like eagles. They will run and not grow weary. They will walk and not faint" (Isaiah 40:31).

God is able to empower you to cast down imaginations, and every high thing that exalts itself against the knowledge of God, and bring into captivity every thought to the obedience of Christ and to think on things which are godly and praiseworthy when negative thoughts show up in your spirit and mind.

Additionally, confess your sins to God and repent and plead the blood of Jesus against every negative thought. Ask God to increase your faith in Him to trust and believe that He is the only one who can bring transformation and renewal in your mind.

"And the apostles said unto the Lord, increase our faith"

**Luke 17:5**

# Chapter Seven

♦

# DWELL ON THE WORD OF GOD DAILY

♦

"Let the Word of Christ dwell in you richly in all wisdom; teaching and admonishing one another in psalms and hymns and spiritual songs, singing with grace in your hearts to the Lord"

**Colossian 3:16**

Dwelling on the Word of God simply means to live or stay on the Word. Dwelling on the Word of God can also mean that you reflect, and meditate on the Word to gain insight, to discover the mind of God on a particular situation concerning you (Joshua 1:8).

The Word of God is the very platform for which many things were or are built. The Bible makes it clear that, "In the beginning was the Word, and the Word was with God, and the Word was God (John 1:1).

The Word of God is the original manual for living. Every manufacturer of every product will always attach a form of manual to the product before selling it. You cannot operate as a pastor's armour bearer without your manual. It is what we need to chart the phase of our lives as believers and pastor's armour bearers. It is possible to say that the Word of God or the Bible is our actually instruction before we leave the earth.

> "For the Word of God is living and active. Sharper than any double-edged sword, it penetrates even to dividing soul and spirit, joints and marrow; it judges the thoughts and attitudes of the heart"

**Hebrews 4:12**

When we allow God's Word to dwell in our lives, it changes and transforms us into the image of God Himself. It also becomes treasured in our lives. "All Scripture is given by inspiration of God, and is profitable for doctrine, for reproof, for correction, for instruction in righteousness, that the man of God may be complete, thoroughly equipped for every good work" (2 Timothy 3:16).

The Word of God is so powerful to allow us to drop off all negative things that disturbed us at one time, and in many cases, overcame us as a pastor's armour bearer and create calmness in our inner spirit when we meditate on it fully.

> "Do not let this Book of the Law depart from your mouth; meditate on it day and night, so that you may be careful to

do everything written in it. Then you will be prosperous and successful"

**Joshua 1:8**

As a pastor's amour bearer, it is very crucial that you develop the habit of dwelling on the Word of God daily. You cannot do anything without the Word of God. The Word of God is our weapon and we cannot afford to forget to take it onto the battlefield.

As we can see from the Bible passage (Ephesians 6:11-17), we are admonished to value the Word of God more importantly, as pastors' armour bearers because our lives depend on it. That is why Paul the apostle wrote that we should

> "11 Put on the whole armour of God, that ye may be able to stand against the wiles of the devil. 12 For we wrestle not against flesh and blood, but against principalities, against powers, against the rulers of the darkness of this world, against spiritual wickedness in high places. 13 Wherefore take unto you the whole armour of God, that ye may be able to withstand in the evil day, and having done all, to stand. 14 Stand therefore, having your loins girt about with truth, and having on the breastplate of righteousness; 15 And your feet shod with the preparation of the gospel of peace; 16 Above all, taking the shield of faith, wherewith ye shall be able to quench all the fiery darts of the wicked. 17 And take the helmet of salvation, and the sword of the Spirit, which is the Word of God"

**Ephesian 6:11-17**

The Word of God is so powerful and in fact has been compared to a two-edged sword. Some may question why has the Word of God been compared to a "two-edged sword"? Amazingly, the Bible educates us to understand that God's Word has the capacity to reach and transform our individual mind, heart and soul. The Word of God has no limitations attached to it whatsoever. For us to be able to perform our duties as a pastor's armour bearer, then we need to dwell on the Word of God for our life which will enable you to fight against any attack from the enemy's camp especially during church services that the Word being preached will have a free cause in the heart, mind and soul of listeners.

When you allow the Word of God to dwell in you richly, you are able to descend effectively on the devil's opinions surrounding your ministry, church, house fellowship and other departments in the church because the Spirit in the Word of God penetrates the very heart and mind of men and to reveal their intentions and thoughts to you as an armour bearer. This also helps us to change our thinking patterns and behaviours especially when it comes to our duties.

> "For the Word of God is quick, and powerful, and sharper than any two-edged sword, piercing even to the dividing asunder of soul and spirit, and of the joints and marrow, and is a discerner of the thoughts and intents of the heart"

**Hebrews 4:12**

One of the main things the devil hates is the Word of God. That is why the enemy, the devil, always wants to attack your mind from reading and dwelling on the Word of God. I have come to appreciate that the Word of God is very pure, incorruptible, inspired, infallible, living, powerful, sharper than any two-edged sword. The Word of God has that ability to nourishing our mind, soul and spirit and is able to purify your thoughts and imaginations, teach, guide, and direct your everyday life in ministry as a pastor's armour bearer.

In view of these, the devil never stops to attack the Word of God that has been spoken unto us just to bring confusion to our mind and heart.

As an armour bearer, it is very necessary to acknowledge that our God is not the "author of confusion". In 1 Corinthians 14:33, we are advised that, "God is NOT the author of confusion but Satan is." The intention of the enemy (devil) is to shake your faith and confuse you with other things central to the Word of God.

As a pastor's armour bearer, you need to understand that attacks from the devil will always be directed to you and especially your families and loved ones just to move your focus away from God's purpose and agenda for your life and ministry. It is important to know that, you are not better and stronger than your Lord and master Jesus Christ who Himself was tempted and attacked by the evil one during His most difficult moments. Just after Jesus Christ fasted and prayed for 40 days and nights and the whole body was very tired, the enemy showed up to tempt Him. One thing that remains very powerful in my mind is that Jesus Christ reminded Himself of the WORD, "It is written." "But He (JESUS CHRIST) answered and said, it is written, 'Man shall not live by bread alone, but by every Word that proceeds out of the mouth of God'" (Matthew 4:4).

The question here is this: When you are attacked and tempted by the enemy, what do you say? Do you give in to the enemy? Do you remind yourself of the sure Word of God dwelling in your side? The Word of God is a weapon against the attacks of the enemy so use it to your advantage.

Let me assure you that you don't have to worry about the devices of the enemy's attacks that are directed at you as a pastor's armour bearer. God will never allow you to be smitten by your enemies. God's Word is there for you to use anytime and anywhere you feel threatened by the enemy. Your family and loved ones are in the hands of God. You are protected and shielded from those attacks in JESUS NAME.

Personally, I have been under numerous attacks from the enemy (car accidents, strokes, sicknesses, lost my jobs twice in two years, children's social services and many more), simply because I was an armour bearer. Nonetheless, I have not given up and never will I give up in Jesus name. One thing I definitely know for sure is that, when you dedicate your life and services to God and to His ordained servant (TRUE-PASTORS), God will always defend and deliver you from troubles and challenges of life. David said in Psalm 23:4, "Yea, though I walk through the valley of the shadow of death, I will fear no evil: for thou art with me; thy rod and thy staff they comfort me".

The rod and the staff represent the "WORD OF GOD" that he dwelt on daily for his life. That was why he was very confident about his future.

When you begin to dwell on the Word of God daily or spend time with God in His Word, you develop confidence in Him concerning your future. You begin to experience or know without a shadow of doubt that God is with you and you don't have to fear. Storms of life will always come against you or may rise all around you. Limitations, hindrances, abuse and ridicules may come from even some church members who may be desiring to be the pastor's armour bearer.

In view of that, they could be skimming and plotting things against you but I can confidently say to you that those storms will bow.

Dwelling on the Word of God actually builds your faith in Him. Spending quality time with God through His Word, you will discover that the perfect peace of God will begin to come into your life even if there is gross darkness of trouble and pain around you. You will develop the confidence that your God is not dead but still alive working on your behalf.

> "For, behold, the darkness shall cover the earth, and gross darkness the people: but the LORD shall arise upon thee, and His glory shall be seen upon thee"
>
> **Isaiah 60:2**

# Chapter Eight

# TRUST IN THE LORD IN THE FACE OF CHALLENGES

"But those who wait on the LORD shall renew their strength; they shall mount up with wings like eagles, they shall run and not be weary, they shall walk and not faint"

**Isaiah 40:31**

Sometimes life can be full of challenges and hurdles. This can be very stressful for every believer. In view of this, we are encouraged to focus and put our trust in the Lord our God so as to strengthen us through the times of our challenges.

As pastors' armour bearers, we are not exempted from this life's challenges. We need to understand that we are at the battlefield and the devil will not back down or leave us alone. The devil knows that we are the ones supporting the pastor and the ministry through prayer, giving of our resources and time, projecting and promoting the vision of God that has been given to them. He will deplore his hosts to attack us through challenges but if we can trust in the Lord's grace and power, trusting Him wholeheartedly, then we can stand the test of time because His grace will be sufficient for us in Jesus name.

It is very true that sometimes we think that there is a delay in God answering our prayer requests concerning our heart's desire. As a pastors' armour bearer, even though your pastor may come to testify about what the Lord is doing for him and his family and you check your life and there is nothing to testify of, this can be painful and hurting. You may begin to question God as to why things are not happening to you and your family but your pastor is being blessed daily.

Naturally in life, nobody wants to experience adversity, trials, disappointments, sadness, and heartache when they are serving God faithfully and especially serving as pastor's armour bearers. I have come to understand that all these challenges and trials are for our good as God may be testing our faith in trusting in Him. Some of these challenges come to us simply because God is refining us to showcase us to the devil as He did for JOB.

> **"But He knoweth the way that I take: when He hath tried me, I shall come forth as gold"**
>
> **Job 23:10**

However, it is very important that I stress this point: If by any chance you are not experiencing the hand and the blessing of

God in your life as an armour bearer, you need to examine your personal relationship with God and see where you have transgressed against the Will of God and repent. David came to the point where he had to ask God to examine him and search his life if there was any sin in him. "Search me, O God, and know my heart: try me, and know my thoughts" (Psalm 139:23).

Trusting God to examine your heart and thoughts is the best thing that you can do for yourself in order to remain faithful and steadfast in serving Him. He knows the heart and mind of every one of us and if we can recognise the very areas we have wronged Him and confess our sins, He is faithful and just to forgive us of all our sins. "If we confess our sins, he is faithful and just to forgive us our sins, and to cleanse us from all unrighteousness" (1 John 1: 9).

Sometimes, people can be faithful for a short period of time. Standing by your pastor in the house of God demands a great deal of commitment and trust in God. Challenges come to everyone under the sun but it takes your trust and faith in the Lord to remain serving Him regardless of these challenges. It takes that faith in God to trust and know that, "For our light affliction, which is but for a moment, worketh for us a far more exceeding and eternal weight of glory" (2 Corinthian 4:17).

When Abraham was asked by God to sacrifice his son Isaac, in fact it did make sense to him but later he witnessed God's faithfulness when his son was restored to him. To Abraham, it was a challenge but he trusted that God had something more for him.

Moses also did not actually understand why God had to take him through 40 years in the terrible wilderness. Later on, Moses understood why God made him a great leader of the children of Israel in their quest to the land of freedom. What about Joseph? He was also faced by the greatest challenge of his life when his own brothers sold him into slavery; the very people he was sent to check their wellbeing and to provide some food to. They mistreated him so badly that it was a challenge to him as to why he had to go through this. Thanks to be our God. He is able to turn our challenges to championship. He turned Joseph's challenges into leadership and a governor of a foreign country.

What are your challenges in life? Trust and know that your God is an awesome God. He will surely take you through every form of trail and challenge facing you as an armour bearer in Jesus name. Don't get discouraged in the face of challenges that show up in your ministry, family, children, employment or marriage. Trust in Him and He will give you the desire of your heart when you faint not.

Walk by faith and not by the things that show up to challenge you. See them as God sees them. Behold, I am the LORD, the God of all flesh: is there anything too hard for me? (Jeremiah 32:27)

**There is no easy way in facing the challenges of life except through the power of the Word of God through faith.**

Elijah was discouraged because of exhaustion. After a great spiritual victory, when he called down fire from heaven and destroyed all the prophets of Baal, one little woman scared him to death because she threatened to kill him. And he was ready to give up. I have had enough, Lord, he said. Take my life; I am no better than my ancestors (1 Kings 19:4). I find that I am often discouraged after spiritual victories. How about you? Do you often find yourself discouraged just when God has done something wonderful in your life? It's not unusual.

Hannah was discouraged because the deepest desire of her heart had not been given to her. And it was a good and worthy desire – to have a baby that she could give back to the Lord. Downhearted and discouraged, in bitterness of soul Hannah wept much and prayed to the Lord for a baby (1 Samuel 1).

Some of you are discouraged because of unfulfilled desires. Maybe it's the desire to be married, but the right person hasn't come along. Maybe, like Hannah, it's the desire to have a baby, but your womb has been closed so far. Maybe it's your dreams of serving God in some special way, but the door hasn't opened yet. It can be discouraging. So, we can certainly see that discouragement is nothing new; it's been around since the beginning of time.

Naomi was discouraged because of financial difficulties and terrible losses. Her husband and two sons had both died, and she was left penniless and homeless. Don't call me Naomi, she told her friends. Call me Mara (meaning bitter), because the Almighty has made my life very bitter (Ruth 1:20-21). It's easy enough to understand her discouragement. Financial difficulties cause a great deal of discouragement for many of us.

Mary and Martha were discouraged because they lost someone they loved, and they had really expected Jesus to save him. After all, Jesus had been healing all kinds of other people; surely He would come and save His beloved friend, Lazarus, they reasoned. And when He didn't, they were very discouraged; Jesus had disappointed them. Lord, Martha said to Jesus, if you had been here, my brother would not have died (John 11:21).

Have you ever set an agenda out for the Lord, expecting Him to work on your timetable, and then been disappointed when He didn't come through? That can be discouraging.

Peter was discouraged because of his own failure. After he denied the Lord three times, Peter went out and wept bitterly, we are told. I imagined he felt that he had blown it for good, and he must have been terribly discouraged with himself. How could he deny the Lord, the One he promised never to deny? When I look at myself and see how inadequate I am, how often I fail, how I go back and do the same things over and over that I know I shouldn't do, I get very discouraged. In fact, that discourages me probably more than anything else. How about you?

Jesus – even Jesus fought discouragement when His friends failed Him; when He was misunderstood; when He tried to help and His help was refused. That really hurts; when you have totally good motives, and yet people don't approve or understand or support you. In fact, they may reject you, as they did Jesus. Well, it is encouraging to see that even these great people of God went through times of discouragement.

God understands discouragement; discouragement is a normal and unavoidable emotion that we must all deal with. It comes to us in different ways, for different reasons, and at different times, but rest assured that the grace of God is sufficient for us in times of discouragement and He will surely see us through when we faint not.

# Chapter Nine

♦

# MAINTAIN THE SPIRIT OF THANKSGIVING

♦

1 Thessalonians 5: 18; Ephesians 5: 20; Philippians 4: 6; Colossians 33: 17

Developing the attitude of gratitude means to have a lifestyle of thanksgiving and able to show appreciation to someone who you revere so highly for what they have done for you. Your attitude remains the same irrespective of the circumstances facing you.

> "Develop an attitude of gratitude, and give thanks for everything that happens to you, knowing that every step forward is a step toward achieving something bigger and better than your current situation."
>
> BRIAN TRACY

You still appreciate God for the very life you have.

Your attitude is that no matter what limitations before you, you will make your mind up to remain grateful. Sometimes negative thoughts and ideas may arise to challenge your love for God but you develop the habit to remain thankful at all times.

## In everything give thanks, for this is the will of God in Christ concerning you

> "Let the high praises of God be in their mouth, and a two-edged sword in their hand, to execute vengeance upon the heathen, and punishments upon the people, to bind their kings with chains, and their nobles with fetters of iron, to execute upon them the judgments written, this honour have all his saints, praise ye the Lord"
>
> **Psalm 149:6-9**

John Henry Newman once said, "I will trust Him whatever, wherever I am, I can never be thrown away. If I am in sickness, my sickness may serve Him, in perplexity, my perplexity may serve Him, if l am in sorrow, my sorrow may serve Him. My sickness or perplexity or sorrow may be necessary causes of some great end, which is quite beyond us. He does nothing in vain."

> ❝
> **"Seeds of discouragement will not grow in a thankful heart."**
>
> ANONYMOUS

According to Joel 1:1-2, "The vine is dried up, and the fig tree languisheth, the pomegranate tree, the palm tree also, and the apple tree, even all the tress of the field, are withered, because joy is withered away from the sons of men."

When we lack the spirit of thankfulness and praises to God for the things that we have now, the little things we even have are taken away from us. Anything we may set our hands on may become dried up. This may consequently lead to the lack of freshness in our marriages and other ramifications of our lives simply because we lack joy and gratitude.

It is very important that we maintain the heart of gratitude always as it brings things faster to us.

The Bible says, "The joy of the Lord is my strength." My bishop once made a statement which really cracked up my brain. According to him, "Gratitude is a covenant attitude"; which is very true. Given that we are children of the Great Jehovah, we have a covenant with Him regarding our salvation. Therefore, it is just important and prudent that we maintain the covenant attitude of gratitude towards Him with the appreciation that God is still and always in control (Luke 12:22-23).

A joyful attitude or thanksgiving brings things our way even if we do not seem to qualify for them. It is my personal observation that when we lose our sense of gratitude, we can lose our peace and joy, for our God desires we enjoy peace and joy at all times (Romans 8: 28).

As David puts it: "I will praise the name of God with a song; I will magnify Him with thanksgiving. This will please the Lord more than an ox or a bull with horns and hoofs; Let the oppressed see it and be glad. You, who seek God, let your hearts revive" (Psalm 69: 30-32).

The accounts of Paul and Silas as recorded in Acts 16: 23-26 is quite revealing. "And when they had laid many stripes upon them, they cast them into prison, charging the jailor to keep them safely, who having received such a charge thrust them into the inner prison, and made their feet fast in the stocks. And at midnight Paul and Silas prayed and sang praises unto God, and the prisoners heard them and suddenly there was a great earthquake, so that the foundations of the prison were shaken, and immediately all the doors were opened, and every one's bands were loosed."

Paul and Silas as we are told were arrested and put in prison for casting a spirit of divination out of a girl. They were subjected to severe torture, nevertheless, in the midst of these suffering and pains, they prayed and sang praises to God. This may sound ridiculous and strange to the other prisoners who were used to hearing only groans and cries of beaten and tortured prisoners.

In the process of time the earthquake that shook the foundations of the prison flung its doors opened with the bonds of not only Paul and Silas released, but equally those of the other enemies.

A question that may come to mind may be what had caused the prison doors to open? Surely, praise and worship is the answer.

Praise and worship lifts us to the presence of God

"There is fullness of joy in the presence of God"

**Deuteronomy 4: 29**

It is important that we recognise the presence of God who created all that we have and will ever need. Paul and Silas no doubt were conscious and aware of the power of praise and worship, how to lift their hearts above their challenges or problems and enter into the presence and power of the Almighty God. Hence, they engaged God's power through praise and worship which brought them into his peace and presence, opening the door of opportunity for the heavenly Father to operate in their circumstances.

The Bible makes it clear that God inhabits in the praises of His people (Psalm 22: 3). In other words, God 'dwells' in the atmosphere of praises. Thus praise is not merely a reaction to coming into the presence of our Maker, but is a vehicle of faith which brings us in to the presence and power of Great Jehovah. Praise and worship is a 'gate pass' which allows us entry into the sacredness of His glory.

The psalmist will say, "Enter into His gates with thanksgiving and into His courts with praise, be thankful unto Him, and bless His name" (Psalm 100:4).

Our Lord and Saviour Jesus Christ also emphasises the need to value the presence of God when it comes to praise and worship; For where two or three are gathered together in my name, there I am in their midst" (Matthew 18: 20). It is also important that whenever we gather to praise His name, our God should be our only main focus of everything we preach and sing about. "I will declare thy name unto my brethren, in the midst of the church will l sing and praise unto thee" (Hebrew 2:12).

It is interesting to note that miracles can manifest in the atmosphere of praise and worship as God's power responds when we invoke His presence into our lives through this medium.

Praising God actually means, "to command, applaud or magnify" – It is an expression of worship, lifting up and glorifying the living Lord. It is an act of humility and focusing our attention upon the Lord, with all our heartfelt expressions of love, adoration and thanksgiving. High praises bring our spirits into the pinnacle of fellowship and intimacy between God and His children.

Praises magnify our awareness of our spiritual union with the highest God, and transports us into the realm of the supernatural, which is in the presence of the power of the Almighty. Therefore when gratitude springs up in the human heart towards God, He is magnified as the worthy source of our blessings and acknowledged as the giver and a glorious Father.

There are several actions involved in praising God. This can consist of verbal expression of adoration, praise and thanksgiving, singing, playing of instruments, dancing and lifting or clapping of hands However, true praise is not merely going through these emotions.

Jesus spoke about the hypocrisy of the Pharisees, whose worship was only outward display and lip service, rather than indication of genuine expression of their love for the faithfulness of our living God "These people draweth nigh unto me with their mouth, and honoureth me with their lips, but their heart is far from me" (Matthew 15: 8).

I have come to realise that a genuine praise to God is a matter of humility and sincere devotion to the Lord with true heart. And as the psalmist will say, "Enter into His gates with thanksgiving, and into His courts with praise. Be thankful to Him and bless His holy name, for the Lord is good" (Psalm 100: 4-5).

The secret key is that if you ever want anything from God, you will have to thank and acknowledge Him for what He has already provided; this is what is known and called faith. The problem with us is that we are mostly very quick to ask God for His help, but just slow to offer thanks unto Him for the provisions He so generously provides us. The Bible succinctly emphasises the importance of thanksgiving with its account of the ten lepers. (Luke 17:17-18).

As we need deliverance, we would need to express thankfulness to the Lord for what He has already done, as the book of Philippians 4:6 encourages us not to be anxious for nothing, but in everything by prayer and supplication, with thanksgiving, let our requests be known to God.

## Praise to God is a Lifestyle

All too often, praise to God is something that many people leave at church, as they see it as event that should only happen when they come together in fellowship with other believers or Christians.

However, praise should be a part and parcel of the believer's lifestyle and as part of their daily prayer life – In the car, at home, be it in the kitchen, bedroom, bathroom and indeed, at all times and places as praise to the Lord brings about the refreshing of the Lord's presence, along with His power and anointing. "…I will bless the Lord at all times, His praise shall continually be in my mouth" (Psalm 34:1).

Praise is an expression of faith, and a declaration of victory. It declares the believer's deep acknowledgement of his divine authority and sovereignty over all our circumstances (Romans 8:28).

Praise is a "sacrifice" that we offer to God voluntarily for the faith we have in His being and for the abundance of His kind mercies and grace; but not just out of fun, "By Him therefore let us offer the sacrifice of praise to God continually, that is, the fruit of our lips giving thanks to His name" (Hebrew 13:15).

### Your Enemies are Dealt with by God Through Praise

Since praise manifests God's presence, we must also realise that praise repels the presence of the enemy, Satan. An atmosphere filled with sincere praise and worship of God by humble, devoted, committed and contrite hearts disgust the devil. He fears and will flee from the power and the presence of the Almighty God.

> "Whoso offereth praise glorifieth me, and to him that ordereth his conversation alright will l show the salvation of God"
>
> **Psalm 50:23**

When the children of Judah found themselves outnumbered by the hostile armies of Ammon, Moab and Mount Seir, King

Jehoshaphat and all the people sought the Lord for His help. The Lord assured the people that this would be His battle and told them to go out against them, and that He would do the fighting for them.

So what did the children of Judah do? Being the people of praise-giving Judah actually means, "Praise", and knowing that God manifests His power through praise and worship, they sent their armies against the enemy, led by praise singers, declaring; "Praise the Lord, for His mercy endureth forever."

The eminent result or the consequences of their actions is well recorded in 2 Chronicles 20:22. When God's people begin to praise His name, it sends the enemy running.

I challenge you to become a person of praise and you will experience the release of the power of God in an awesome way. God gives us assurances of additional blessings as we praise Him. When we praise God, He honours us as His children, provides His loving divine protection and divine covering (2 Samuel: 22: 47-51). Our failure to praise the Lord leaves us out of His loving divine protection and divine covering hence we become exposed to the vagaries of the enemy (1 Samuel 2: 27-32).

You may be familiar with that wonderful and exciting chorus, Under The Canopy of God... if you do as I do, come along and begin to praise the great Jehovah now. May God richly bless you for this praises. Our praise can also serve as a testimony or witness to those who do not know the Lord (1 Peter 2:9); for the Lord our God works miraculously through praises.

## Thankfulness Encourages and Motivates People

Thankfulness is contagious. It is a fact of life that whatever we do sets example for other people. Thus if we fail to show a thankful heart to our God by our actions, we may become stumbling blocks to other people. This explains why believers would need to demonstrate high degrees of commitment, devotion and seriousness of attitude during praise and worship sessions at all times.

Today, in our church we have a devoted full service purposely for thanksgiving, praise and worship. The testimonies of this session are abundant; amongst others is the resulting regularisation of the immigration status of those members of the congregation who placed their needs of indefinite leave to remain in the United Kingdom before the Almighty God.

We have set an atmosphere of praise and worship which impacts heavily on our new members and even first-time visitors as they are able to testify to the lifting up of their spirits before the Lord and their feeling of being blessed.

My personal testimony is the realisation that when thanksgiving is practically demonstrated, such as evangelism, it blesses others and sets examples for those around us.

## Thankfulness Strengthens Your Faith

"Rooted and built up in Him and established in the faith, as ye have been taught, abounding therein with thanksgiving"

**Colossian 2:7**

Thanksgiving is so powerful that it lifts up your faith and encourages others. The Word of God says that, without faith, it is impossible to please God. In this sense, thankfulness may be seen as the fuel to faithfulness, as it strengthens the faith of the believer and his/her dependence on the Lord for all their provisions.

## GOD IS ALL YOU NEED TO HAVE ALL YOUR NEEDS MET ADEQUATELY

You may have been feeling defeated. It could be because you have forgotten the benefits of God through thanksgiving (Habakkuk 3:17-18; Joel 1;1-2). "You shall know the truth and the truth shall set you free."

Let God's Word tell you who you are and what you have. Don't give attention to anyone who tells you anything different for God's Word is true. When God called Gideon a mighty warrior, there was no evidence to suggest that it was true. God saw and spoke about what will become. Learn and understand what God says about you and accept His opinion about you. Believe what God says about whom you are in Christ Jesus, and you will become just what you are in Him. By faith through thanksgiving, believe the truth and act on what you believe. You will build your faith as you constantly remind yourself of whom you are in Christ Jesus.

### Thankfulness is the fuel that sustains your faith.

Develop the attitude to be thankful to God always because thankful people always have their tanks full of God's blessings and divine favour.

# Chapter Ten

# DON'T GIVE UP ON YOUR MINISTRY

In the early stages of pregnancy, a baby is likely to be lost. This also applies to our God-given dream; therefore we need to protect it and ensure it is preserved. The enemy tried so hard to destroy Moses and Jesus before they reached their second birthday. The question is why? Simply because the enemy feared their future and he fears your future too.

In addition, when a prospective mother is pregnant, she has to do certain things in order to deliver what God has promised her. Others may do other things negative to protect that baby. Therefore you may ask; why do some pregnant women still drink alcoholic beverage, smoke and eat certain types of food and you cannot do the same? The answer is that what you are carrying is different from what they are carrying. Your dream is different from theirs.

Remember that pursuing your dream requires daring to be different; even some radical, but you have to do it to see your dream come true.

Sometimes it will demand that you disconnect from some relationships and habits that can hurt you. It will also require you to stay out of certain places and reordering your priorities according your God-given destiny, not popular consent.

**The future is created by those who don't have everyone as a friend.**

> "Never give up, for that is just the place and time that the tide will turn"
> 
> HARRIET BEECHER STOWE.

Esther's vision meant that she decided to put her life on the line and say, "If perish, I perish." She did not perish even though she was willing to die for her vision.

It is sometimes shocking to know that some people wear themselves out trying to fulfil a vision God did not give them. They do this just to win or demonstrate that they are as talented as their peers, brothers, sisters and sometimes their parents.

> "Never underestimate the power of dreams and the influence of the human spirit."
> 
> WILMA RUDOLPH

When you look at Abraham's life, he had to learn a hard lesson when God promised him a son. He was so impatient with God and was worried about getting old. He took a bad decision following a bad advice and ended up fathering Ishmael. As my bishop always says, "Bad choices always lead to bad decisions; the choices you make in life are either making or breaking you." Abraham had to live with the outcome of his decision for the rest of his life.

Furthermore, people who make this mistake end up with the sense of failure and frustration because they are constantly measuring themselves by somebody else's assignment. It is very important that each and every one of us identifies our individual talents and gifts concerning our dreams. Remember that a man's gifts are what bring him before great men and open doors for him. Be strong in the Lord and strive to see your dreams come true.

> **"Nothing is as potent as a focused life."**
> UNKNOWN

It is clear that without a clear purpose in life, one can only be changing directions, jobs, relationships, churches, etc., hoping that each change they make will make them settle. This is a pure lack of focus. The power of focusing can be seen in a light. Scientists have discovered that with a magnifying glass, the rays of the sun can set paper on fire. But when the light is focused even more as a laser beam, it can cut through steel.

In Philippians 3:13-14, Paul made it clear that, "Brethren, I do not count myself to have apprehended; but one thing I do, forgetting those things which are behind and reaching forward to those things which are ahead. 14 I press toward the goal for the prize of the upward call of God in Christ Jesus."

We discovered here that Paul was very obsessed in focusing on his dream by making Christ known to the world. Therefore if we want our lives to be impactful, then we all need to remain focused on our dreams. We need to be very disciplined to remain focused and not get distracted by winds of doctrine.

Sometimes our fellow brother or sister can see something in us that we may be doing wrong. Don't get upset. Be honest and ask yourself, could they be right, then pray to God and start on your road to making changes that will make you a better person for yourself as well as for God.

Watch, stand fast in the faith, be brave, and be strong. This is what 1 Corinthians 16:13 (NKJV) says. As Christians striving to live our lives the way God wants us to live our lives, we always have to be watchful as to the many ways of sin that are all around us. We have to stand fast and resist the desire to fall into the traps that the enemy is trying to set for us.

Every day we should acknowledge to God that we need Him. When we start to act like we do not need God in our lives and that we can do everything ourselves, that's when we run into problems. The next time we are about to do something, acknowledge God and watch Him make your situation better.

We have to realise what our purpose is in God. Only when we do that can our lives take on a new meaning and we start to work towards the destiny that God has for us.

A pastor once said that new levels bring new devils. When God wants us to move forward in His love and to learn more about Him and His son Jesus Christ, the devil doesn't like it nor wants us to move forward, so you start to see negative situations come up.

In the pursuit of destiny, many things may catch your eyes but keep your single eye on the very purpose for your life. Focusing on your past histories or background will only hinder your future. No matter how long and depressing the past was, just look ahead. People may be calling you by your past, family members may be reminding you of your bad behaviours during your childhood stages, but I can guarantee you that you are more than what they think they know. Your days of tears will be over soon. "For His anger endureth but a moment; in His favour is life: weeping may endure for a night, but joy cometh in the morning" (Psalm 30:5).

"And the work of righteousness shall be peace; and the effect of righteousness, quietness and assurance forever" (Isaiah 37:17).

"Fear not; for thou shalt not be ashamed: neither be thou confounded; for thou shalt not be put to shame: for thou shalt forget the shame of thy youth, and shalt not remember the reproach of thy widowhood anymore" (Isaiah 54:4).

I want to assure you that any form of reproach or anything, be they rejections, regrets, disappointments, failures, you name them, which cause you to weep, the Lord God is contending on your behalf and you will hold your peace in JESUS NAME.

The Lord is saying to you right now that you are His battle axe and weapons of war: for with you will He break in pieces the nations, and with you will He destroy kingdoms (Jeremiah 51:20). Just remain focused in Jesus name.

No matter where you have been, no matter where you are at this moment, if have not found God's plan for your life; please stop what you are doing and start looking for it and begin where you are right now. God is ready to put your life back on track. He is ready to give you a sense of hope. "For I know the thoughts that I think toward you, saith the LORD, thoughts of peace, and not of evil, to give you an expected end" (Jeremiah 29:11).

It is only God-given hope that can sustain us through those difficult and trial times. You may be wondering in your mind that, "Am I ever going to get to my destiny? Why have I not married yet? Why are others getting good jobs and are building houses in the village and you have not even asked for a price of bricks?" Well, the good news is that God is preparing you for something great.

The word of God says that, "Though it tarries, wait for it, for it will surely come, and will not tarry" (Habakkuk 2:3).

We need to understand that everything has their moment and cycle in an hour and some in a century; but the very purpose of that particular thing (dreams, plans, education, child birth, etc.) shall surely complete their cycle whether long or short. God's purposes and plans for your life will not be cut off but will surely come to pass in your life.

Brethren; instead of focusing on our problems, it is very important that we look to our God and trust His Word. The

Bible encourages us that, "Many are the afflictions of the righteous: but the Lord delivereth him out of them all" (Psalm 34:19). Also, Isaiah 43:2 says, "When thou passest through the waters, I will be with thee; and through the rivers, they shall not overflow thee: when thou walkest through the fire, thou shalt not be burned; neither shall the flame kindle upon thee."

> "If you stay focused and right on track, you will get to where you want to be."
> **UNKNOWN**

Praise God. There is hope for you as you serve faithfully (Job 14:9).

# Chapter Eleven

♦

# STAY AWAY FROM TOXIC RELATIONSHIPS

♦

"He who walks with the wise grows wise, but a companion of fools suffers harm"

**Proverbs 13:20**

Who do we call a toxic relationship?

A toxic relationship is a relationship that is very detrimental to your life, existence in ministry, family and your pastor. These individuals come into your life and affect your relationship with your man of God (PASTOR) and sometimes make you lose your identity and calling in ministry. Toxic relationships are those that come into your life just to drain the happiness of your service out of your life. These personalities will do everything to impose their negative way of life on you just to move you away from your appointed place of blessing. As you allow them around you for a long period of time, they affect the way you look at your ministry and destroy your relationship with your pastor whom you serve faithfully.

Sometimes it can be very difficult to realise some toxic relationships around your ministry. This is why it is very important to choose your friends wisely as a pastor's armour bearer. It is very necessary that you allow only those who are there to motivate, encourage and inspire you to do the work of ministry; not those who will discourage you from serving your pastor and the ministry you find yourself in.

Toxic relationships are the group of individuals who will pollute your mind against your pastor after you have been corrected or rebuked. They are the types of friends who cause division among believers and want you to be a part of them. They are not good for your ministry as a pastor's armour bearer.

We all need people we can trust and depend on to uplift the spirit of God within us especially when we are in difficulties and moments of despair; friends that you can trust and be real with when it comes to your ministry and family.

I have heard my bishop say things like; "No association leaves us neutral". This implies that we cannot escape the influence of those we call friends. Personally, I have keenly observed that we get very close to those we call our friends or associates and most often, we get influenced by these individuals.

In view of this, as a pastor's armour bearer, it is mandatory that we avoid toxic friendships and rather, build our closer relationships with those with whom we agree. In Amos 3:3, the Bible made it clear that, we cannot walk with individuals we do not agree with. "Can two walk together, except they be agreed?" The type of people you surround yourself with actually determine what surrounds or associates with you. The toxic individuals will try to infect your mind with negative thoughts which if not guarded, can creep into your life.

Building great relationships takes time and energy. And you only discover how valuable such relationships are when they are tested. One author writes: "Contouring your heart to beat with another requires extensive whittling, to trim away self-centeredness. Some say that it's like riding the bus; if you are going to have a company you must then be willing to stop over to accommodate other people and the baggage they bring."

Any individual in your life influencing you negatively (ungodly counsels) should never be allowed to remain as a friend. In 2 Samuel 13:1-29, we were told how an individual person's kingship was destroyed just because of toxic friendship. Jonadab was Amnon's best friend and they had lived together for years possibly sharing ideas, dreams, visions, and goals. A time came when Jonadab needed an advice from his so-called friend, Amnon, regarding his future. That one advice actually cost him his future to be a king.

And it came to pass after this, that Absalom the son of David had a fair sister, whose name was Tamar; and Amnon the son of David loved her. And Amnon was so vexed, that he fell sick for his sister, Tamar; for she was a virgin; and Amnon thought it hard for him to do anything to her. But Amnon had a friend, whose name was Jonadab, the son of Shimeah David's brother: and Jonadab was a very subtil man. And he said unto him, Why art thou, being the king's son, lean from day to day? Wilt thou not tell me? And Amnon said unto him, I love Tamar, my brother Absalom's sister. And Jonadab said unto him, Lay thee down on thy bed, and make thyself sick: and when thy father cometh to see thee, say unto him, I pray thee, let my sister Tamar come, and give me meat, and dress the meat in my sight, that I may see it, and eat it at her hand.

So Amnon lay down, and made himself sick: and when the king was come to see him, Amnon said unto the king, I pray thee, let Tamar my sister come, and make me a couple of cakes in my sight, that I may eat at her hand. Then David sent home to Tamar, saying, Go now to thy brother Amnon's house, and dress him meat. So Tamar went to her brother Amnon's house; and he was laid down. And she took flour, and kneaded it, and made cakes in his sight, and did bake the cakes. And she took a pan, and poured them out before him; but he refused to eat. And Amnon said, Have out all men from me. And they went out every man from him. And Amnon said unto Tamar, Bring the meat into the chamber that I may eat of thine hand. And Tamar took the cakes which she had made, and brought them into the chamber to Amnon her brother. And when she had brought them unto him to eat, he took hold of her, and said unto her, come lay with me, my sister....... The story continued.

This is the main reason why you need to be careful of those you allow into your life as friends. Any friendship that does not add to you, increase, appreciate, establish or multiply you but subtracts, makes life worse to you or leads to all forms of failure should be cut off. It does not matter how long the friendship has been. You are safer breaking that friendship before your life is broken down alongside your health.

> "Friendship is a choice you make and not legally demanded."
> FERDINAND S LAWSON

Be open and frank with such toxic friends and let them know that you cannot get anywhere with their negative influences in your life. Remember that such toxic friendships are like a car with flat tyres. You cannot go anywhere until you change those tyres.

Who is the friend in your life that you share your dreams and ideas with? Whatever the case may be, you need to be very careful because it could really cost you your destiny. In Proverbs 18:24, Solomon said, "There is a friend who sticks closer than a brother." Relationship is about quality; not quantity. That is why heart connection can be so much stronger than blood connections when it comes to relationships.

Whatever you do, try as much as possible to stay away from these toxic friendships or relationships around your ministry. Staying away from toxic relationships or friendships means that you have the responsibility to clear or avoid relationships that may

> "Any friendship void of agreement is 100% subject to lack of achievement in life."
> FERDINAND S LAWSON

or have negative influences on your life and hinder you from getting to your destiny. When it comes to your purpose in life, you need to actually search for those people who may discourage you from your assignment in life and avoid them completely.

It is very important to know that people you call friends are very necessary in achieving your purpose in life or they could lead to the destruction of your destiny. They are either adding to you or subtracting from you. They are either making your life better or making it worse. You decide the types of friendship you want to keep or to avoid in order to get to your sure destiny.

"A righteous person is cautious with friendship, but the way of the wicked leads them astray"

**Proverbs 12: 26**

> "People in our lives are like buttons in an elevator which take us up to the top floor, keep us on the ground or to the basement."
>
> **BISHOP MICHAEL HUTTON- WOOD**

To be able to overcome the limitations to destiny, it is crucial to take your time and assess the types of friendship you have in your life. If there are friends or relationships that regularly affect your productivity emotionally and sometimes having impact on your health, it is about time you decide to keep them or get rid of them completely so as to get to your sure future.

In Psalm 1:1, we are admonished not to even walk with them. "Blessed is the man that walketh not in the counsel of the ungodly, nor standeth in the way of sinners, nor sitteth in the seat of the scornful."

You must avoid the company of those people who do not in any way share your vision or have your interest at heart. You must do everything to protect and preserve your destiny. God has a purpose, a plan, and a bright and greater future for you. This is why you must not allow negative people to sow seeds of discouragement in your life and distract you from God's divine purpose.

It is not easy to stay away from so-called friends but my fellow believer; it will be to your best interest to do whatever you can to stay away from them. A negative individual or friend has the tendency to influence your character and behaviours. "Birds of the same feathers flock together."

Interestingly, you cannot actually determine the outcome of a relationship as to whether that person in your life as a friend will continue to remain the dependable and reliable individual as you first met them. However, most often than not, it is not very easy to identify any destructive friendship but it is good to be aware of this possibility.

As you decide to overcome the things that hinder you from reaching your goals in life, it is also vital to be aware of those friends that set themselves as negative critics in your life. These individuals could be limiting you by reminding you of your past mistakes and shortfalls.

> "Now I beseech you, brethren, mark them which cause divisions and offences contrary to the doctrine which ye have learned; and avoid them. For they that are such serve not our Lord Jesus Christ, but their own belly; and by good words and fair speeches deceive the hearts of the simple"

**Romans 16:17-18**

It is important that you treat people the same way you would like them to treat you. You need to see and assess the benefits of your friends in your life. Whatever the case, each and every one of us needs friends in our lives. No one is an island and never will be. We need friends that will help us get to our destiny and are willing to accommodate us during the good and the bad times.

Therefore these are the types of relationship or friendship that you need in your life. You actually need a friend that will enable you and empower you to make good decisions regarding crucial moments in your life. Wouldn't you want a good friend to lift you up when you have fallen into the gutter?

> "Iron sharpeneth iron; so a man sharpeneth the countenance of his friend"
> 
> **Proverbs 27:17 KJV**

When it comes to your achievements in life, there will also be different kinds of individuals who will be attracted to you. These people can be classified as pilot friends, first class friends, and economy friends determining your flight in life.

## The Pilot Friendship

These kinds of individuals are friends in your life serving as mentors giving you speed in whatever you do. They board your friendship flight to motivate you, encourage and sometimes take the ultimate responsibility to ensure that you achieve your dreams. A pilot friend adds value to you and propels you to get to that sure goal that you have set for yourself. They share your vision and sometimes will go all the way to stay with you until you become all that God has made you to be. They never leave you along the way regardless of your mistakes. They actually see great treasure in you and bring the gold out of you.

Remember that this kind of individuals in your life do not spy on you but are always there to celebrate your successes. They are very concerned about your failures because they can see the greatness in your life and will go all the way to encourage you to get to the top. Pilot friends know your weaknesses but will not remind or dwell on those negative past or limit your progress in the pursuit of your dreams. Rather, they show you your strengths even in the midst of fearful events just to fortify your faith, and free your spirit whenever there is anxiety. They do not leave you in the mid-air. They become your pillar in life.

## First Class Friendship

These types of friends also gravitate toward you simply because you share the same vision with them. They only stay with you as long as they can get something from you. However, sometimes, when situations get worse and things are not getting the way they think they should be, they get offended and give all kinds of excuses to stay away from you, even though they share the same vision with you. They have different agendas regarding the fulfilment of those dreams and will only give you limited information as to what to do to achieve God's purpose for your life.

## The Economy Friendship

Economy friends are those who come into your life because of what you can only give them to manage their own life. They do not add value to you but are always there to collect and receive from you. Although they also share your vision, they will not be happy if you are doing better than them. They will do everything possible to keep you in the same economy class. They are only happy for you as long as you remain in the economy level until you decide to do something productive with your life. They will say things like we are all managing life here and now you are saying that you have to move on in life. They will frustrate you from moving higher in life.

Even though you are thinking positive to remain focused on your assignment in life, these individuals will have negative ideas about you. You need to keep a positive attitude even when you are in the midst of these friends. Develop and establish defence mechanisms or boundaries to create your own happiness when you are around these toxic friends.

Additionally, toxic friends do not only limit themselves, they also limit the progress of people around them. They also cease to add value or contribution to the friendship that you have with them and cause division among you and other productive friends that are willing to come into your life. Stay away from them.

> "Life is not built on selfishness and self-centeredness; it's built on productive and relevant relationships."
>
> **FERDINAND S LAWSON**

# Chapter Twelve

## CATCH YOUR PASTOR'S SPIRIT

"And he said, Thou hast asked a hard thing: nevertheless, if thou see me when I am taken from thee, it shall be so unto thee; but if not, it shall not be so. And it came to pass, as they still went on, and talked, that, behold, there appeared a chariot of fire, and horses of fire, and parted them both asunder; and Elijah went up by a whirlwind into heaven. And Elisha saw it, and he cried, my father, my father, the chariot of Israel, and the horsemen thereof. And he saw him no more: and he took hold of his own clothes, and rent them in two pieces. He took up also the mantle of Elijah that fell from him, and went back, and stood by the bank of Jordan"

**2 Kings 2:10-13 KJV**

## The company you keep in life determines what accompanies you in life

As my bishop's armour bearer and having walked with him for many years, I have come to discover that when you walk closely with your man of God, the anointing and the spirit of your pastor will surely rub on you. One of the benefits or blessings of walking closely with the pastor you served faithfully is that you will gain more knowledge and insight of him/her. You will know him/her better, because you will hear them speak over and over your life. The disciples of Jesus Christ were able to do more because they followed Him faithfully and caught the spirit operating on Him. They were loyal and devoted to Him.

Therefore, as your pastor's armour bearer, if you can humble and serve faithfully with the heart of loyalty, the spirit of your pastor will automatically come on you. The Bible gave account that, "Joshua, son of Nun, was filled with the spirit of wisdom because Moses had laid his hands on him. So the Israelites listened to him and did what the LORD had commanded Moses" (Deuteronomy 34:9).

Nothing flows towards you without a connection. In this case, your connectivity to your pastor will determine what level of their spirit will flow to you in life and in ministry. Loyalty and faithfulness are the catalysts that activate the spirit of your pastor to increase in your life. Scripture has given us an incredible insight of how walking faithfully with a man of God can actually open you up for some supernatural miracles in your life.

We have also learnt a lesson from the lives of Elisha and Elijah as they walked together in faith and how Elisha caught double measures of his master, leader, pastor (ELIJAH). I have come to understand that it takes desire and perseverance to catch the spirit and the anointing on your pastor. Elisha understood this principle and pursued his master to the point of him leaving the earth because of the relationship he had with him. I have experienced some positive things in my life simply because I have developed the attitude to follow and pursue faithfully and remained loyal to my bishop; who I see as my spiritual and destiny father in my area of ministry.

Yes, sometimes, there may be some few challenges here and there but it does not stop me from serving faithfully bearing in mind that we are all humans and offenses come at times ( Luke 17:1). There is a greater reward in heaven and on earth for those who serve the servants of God faithfully (Hosea 12:13).

> "Whoever welcomes a prophet as a prophet will receive a prophet's reward, and whoever welcomes a righteous person as a righteous person will receive a righteous person's reward"
>
> **Matthew 10:41**

## FIVE PRINCIPLES FOR CATCHING YOUR PASTOR'S SPIRIT

Principles are fundamental guidelines that enable, promote, enhance and shape the value and behaviour of a person. From my field of work, principle serves as a professional code of conduct, ethical behaviour that is necessary for treating people fairly regardless of their race, colour, etc. Let me share some few principles that you need to develop and have in order to catch and flow in the spirit on your pastor.

## PRINCIPLE ONE: WORKING WITH YOUR PASTOR

I have observed that some few armour bearers don't understand the importance of working with their pastors to fulfil God's agenda and vision for the ministry they serve. Some even think that working with their pastor to achieve their purpose is going to limit, stop or prevent them from achieving the plans and ambitions they have for themselves.

I can boldly say to these individuals that, it can never be true. I have served my bishop for many years and still being fulfilled in my ministry of writing, education, work and family. Until you understand how God works, you cannot lay your life down for another man in the area of service. Little did I know that I had writing skills within me until I started working with my bishop by carrying his books and operating them at various book stands.

Sometimes, I drove him at odd hours without complaining, not knowing that I was nurturing my skill of writing indirectly. By the grace of God, this is my sixth book within two years because my bishop has the spirit of writing and has written 19 books in two years. The spirit of your pastor gives you speed in achieving greater things in life if you serve faithfully and work with them in love. This is to say that, "You need a father to father you, to grow feathers, to fly further than your father flew in life." Without a role model in your life, you cannot play your roles well.

Some pastors' armour bearers have lost the commitment in serving for a long haul in the churches they served simply because of the fear of not accomplishing their personal dreams and aspirations. In view of that, they do not dedicate fully to the vision and dreams of their pastors. They have forgotten that, "knowing that whatsoever good thing any man doeth, the same shall he receive of the Lord, whether he be bond or free" (Ephesian 6:8).

The principle here is the willingness to work diligently with your pastor to fulfil God's mandate on his/her life and the ministry. By so doing, your dreams and goals are unfolded in Jesus name. We can see from the above scripture that, brother Elisha had to work hard for the double portions. Until you are willing to sacrifice your time, plans and desires to work with your pastor, you cannot catch the spirit on them. One of the things that amazes me is that, Elisha came to the realisation that, to be able to catch and reap the full anointing/spirit on his master, he had to sow the seed of sacrifice to harvest the double portions. It is my fervent and earnest prayer that pastors' armour bearers will develop and understand the principle of working with their pastors to fulfil God's mandate for their respective churches through the pastors God has given them.

## PRINCIPLE TWO: PURSUIT OF YOUR PASTOR'S ANOINTING

You can't catch or capture the spirit on your father until you chase him. Our Lord Jesus told His disciples to follow him and he would make them fishers of men (Matthew 4:19). This simply means that until you follow, pursue, or chase an individual, you cannot catch or receive what is on them.

To be able to function and have the rod of your pastor working in your hands, you need to pursue with intention to capture God's anointing on your pastor. Until you follow or devote your attention with the hope of attracting and gaining the measure of that anointing on your pastor faithfully, his ROD will not work in your hands. This is the main reason why it is very necessary that those who follow or surround themselves with their pastor must develop the mind-set of pursuit.

You can only know the heart and catch the spirit of the one you follow faithfully. Elisha understood the principle of pursuit in order to catch the anointing on his master, Elijah. He also saw the need in his life that, very soon, his master would be leaving the earth and for him to operate like his master, he had to pursue to the last.

### In life, what you are not willing to pursue, you are permitted to possess.

As a pastor's armour bearer, there will be a time that people will do things to distract your intention to follow your pastor with all your heart, but you need to understand that following or pursuing to catch your pastor's anointing will demand your total focus than your skill or ability.

As you pursue the anointing on your pastor, you will have to overcome the negative experiences, disappointments, rejections, treatments failures and pains you may go through. Sometimes, you may not even be sure of the outcome of following your pastor after you have left your family and work to see your pastor's dream come to reality. However, if you can focus on your pastor like Elisha did until they got to the mountain, you will experience or have the "double portion" of your pastor's anointing in Jesus name.

### You will never have anything until you have a burning desire for it.

You have to do the ridiculous to experience the miraculous. Elisha followed with all his life and he obtained the double portion of Elijah's anointing. Remember also that, the anointing of a pastor cannot be entrusted to complacent armour bearers. In order to catch the anointing on your pastor, you need to develop the spirit of obedience. From the book, Raising Spiritual Sons, by Dr. John A. Tetsola, he explains that spiritual sons are those who obey God and follow His instructions even though that instruction may stretch their obedience of faithfulness.

He explains in his book that, God is going to tell you not to bow before Nebuchadnezzar, but He is not going to tell you if there will be a fourth man in the fire. You must have faith in the God of instructions as you pursue your pastor's heart, even when your logic can't explain it. You must understand that every time God gives you present instructions, He has a future destination on His mind. God never instructs you because of where you are, but because of where you are going.

### PRINCIPLE THREE: REMAIN LOYAL AND FAITHFUL TO YOUR PASTOR

As a pastor's armour bearer, it is important to note that one of the principles of an armour bearer is to remain loyal and faithful to pastors. You are in their lives to promote, protect

> **"Loyalty is the complete support and defences of a leader."**
> **UNKNOWN**

and to preserve the vision of God for the ministry. You are not there to criticise, undermine their leadership, or override their authority in the church regardless of the knowledge you may have in one capacity or the other.

One of the things I have personally observed and do is that, I don't join individuals in the church to speak against my bishop. It is in my best interest to discourage them from speaking negative things about him. Being loyal and faithful to your pastors is a great blessing to them and nothing can substitute this principle. This is because it takes loyal and faithful armour bearers around the pastor to carry some of the burdens so as to encourage the pastor to accomplish God's purpose for the ministry.

Funny enough, I have seen many armour bearers cracked under pressure of loyalty and faithfulness. They excused themselves from church meetings and some even take sabbatical leave (meaning not showing up to do the work they spoke and committed themselves in the first place). In a natural fact, loyalty demands that you remain consistent in

> **"Being faithful in the smallest things is the way to gain, maintain, and demonstrate the strength needed to accomplish something great."**
> **ALEX HARRIS**

standing with your pastor in ministry regardless of good or bad times. The painful thing that can affect a pastor's ministry is when people deject them in difficult moments instead of standing with them to overcome these painful moments of their lives.

"And whatsoever ye do, do it heartily, as to the Lord, and not unto men"

**Colossians 3:23**

One that surprises me is the spirit of loyalty in Joseph. Although he was mistreated and put in prison, he never displayed any sign of disloyalty in service to Pharaoh. I am pretty sure that, Pharaoh himself was shocked at the manner at which Joseph behaved and served to bring his dreams/vision/purpose and agenda into reality (Genesis 41:33-36).

- Do you stand in the defence of your pastors when wrong things are said about them?
- What are the wrong accusations that are being circulated about the ministry and your pastor?

> **"It is the spirit of loyalty to a God-chosen leader that makes promotion possible in your life."**
>
> **FERDINARD LAWSON**

Fellow armour bearer, it is my prayer that you remain loyal and faithful to your pastors during moments of difficulty in their lives and God will surely reward your faithfulness in due season. Develop the attitude and spirit of loyalty and faithfulness.

Stand alongside your pastors and above all, remember that every faithful and loyal servant will increase in grace and blessings (Proverbs 28:20a NASB).

## PRINCIPLE FOUR: RESPECT YOUR PASTOR

It is also very important that as your pastor's armour bearer, you show and demonstrate respect gratefully to your pastor at all times especially during church services or meetings. In Hebrews 13:7, we are admonished not to forget but remember them which have the rule over you, who have spoken unto you the Word of God: whose faith follow. Sometimes disagreements and misunderstandings may occur in the ministry and you may have the right to say or explain things, do not rebuke your pastor and not publicly either.

Whatever be the case, show respect to your pastor in public and find the appropriate time to meet him/her one-on-one to explain your disagreement. If that pastor values your contribution, he or she may thank you for that contribution. Never demand for an apology in public. If possible, remain calm and respectful and loyal to your pastor. In every society or community, people will always say negative things against pastors but it is what you say more about your pastor that others will believe and hold on to.

> "We ask you, brothers, to respect those who labour among you and are over you in the Lord and admonish you, and to esteem them very highly in love because of their work. Be at peace among yourselves. And we urge you, brothers, admonish the idle, encourage the fainthearted, help the weak, be patient with them all"

**1 Thessalonians 5:12-14**

Respecting your pastor also demands that you don't entertain negative comments and insults about them because when you do, you open yourself for destruction and failures (Titus 3:10-11). We also observed in Numbers 12:1-16 that, Miriam and Aaron were punished by God for disrespecting their leader and pastor (Moses). They thought their pastor/leader (Moses) had lost the plot and that he was arrogant. They also thought that His behaviour could serve as a bad example for the children of Israel.

Sometimes, it is not the intention but the how and who you say things to about your pastor. Being a pastor's armour bearer does not give you the platform to disrespect your pastor regardless of the differences that you may have with them. Offences may come but never show disrespect to your head. Encourage others to respect and obey them and learn to forgive your pastor when they offend you (Matthew 5:4; 1 Peter 2:23).

## PRINCIPLE FIVE: TRUSTWORTHY

As an armour bearer, it is very necessary that you can be trusted by your leader (pastor, teacher, apostle, evangelist, prophet) in regards to things pertaining to them or a member of the ministry that you may have heard because of the relationship you have with your leader. A trustworthy armour bearer is someone who can be relied on, and who has cultivated the spirit of loyalty.

To an effective and dynamic armour bearer, your service in the ministry requires that you establish a trustworthy relationship with your leader and the members of your ministry. Trust is characterised as an attitude which involves relying with confidence on someone. Trust is considered as a process and time, reliance on others, risk and fragility are identified as basic attributes of trust. As an armour bearer, most often if not all the time, you will get privileged information just because of the position you are in the life of your leaders/pastors. It is vital that you keep things confidential and your mouth shut.

## Chapter Thirteen

♦

# DON'T DENY YOUR MINISTRY YOUR INVALUABLE INPUT

♦

Your mission in life is the work of God you have been created to do on this planet earth. There is no man born on earth without a purpose or a mission. The question you may be asking is, "How do I discover my mission for life and how to do I become very effective in that mission?"

> "A life without purpose/mission is worse than a cancer."
>
> **FERDINAND LAWSON**

Yes, it is true that some individuals actually work through this world without discovering their God-given mission and therefore live a frustrated life. Some may have discovered it but never did anything to bring that mission to pass in their lives. Fulfilling your mission as an armour bearer is not difficult in the sense that you were born to be it and God's grace is backing you to accomplish this mission or assignment on earth. Your discovery of your mission in life enables you to accomplish a lot for the Kingdom of God without feeling depressed only if you can pray and look enough.

Looking at the life and the mission of our Lord and Saviour, Jesus Christ, His mission was given to Him before He was born. This means that, Jesus Christ's mission on earth was commissioned in heaven and was declared and fulfilled here on earth.

> "Then I said, 'Behold, I come; in the scroll of the book it is written of me. I delight to do your Will, O my God, and your law is within my heart"
>
> **Psalm 40:7-8 NKJV**

One thing I have learnt and discovered over the years of being an armour bearer is that, my mission is designed and commissioned in heaven. Having discovered this, I have developed an attitude that no man can confuse me concerning my mission. This has prevented me from being tossed around by false doctrines and teachings about what and who God has created me for.

When you have a personal revelation about your mission in life, you are fully persuaded to follow it through regardless of the pressure that comes with it; you are determined to ensure that no devil talks you out of that mission that heaven has ordained you to do.

Have you ever asked yourself why some armour bearers excel in their ministry while others fall along the way?

Have you ever wondered the secret and motivation behind Elisha's desire to pursue his master, Elijah, to the point of his departure from this earth?

Elisha foresaw that his mission couldn't be fulfilled until he followed his master to the end and to receive double portion of the grace on his master. I have seen and heard how some pastors' armour bearers give up so easily because of pressure and demands from their pastors/ Consequently, they lose their mission in their pastor's life. Jesus Christ made the disciples to understand that to be great in life, they needed to follow till He made them fishers of men. The disciples knew the importance of their mission and were fully persuaded to follow to become all that God had created them for.

> "The mission you have determines your movement in life."
>
> FERDINARD LAWSON

In fact, many are following their pastors as armour bearers but haven't been called by God. Some are also stepping into the office or ministry of armour bearers without having the confirmation from heaven. The fact that others are doing it and having the privileges to travel or be at meetings with their pastors, especially during great church programs, they think they are called into the ministry of an armour bearer.

Many have fallen or lost their spiritual lives because they were doing things that they were not wired or ordained to do and they get smitten by the pressure and the devil's attacks. Seeing others serving as armour bearers to their pastors does not mean that you are called to step into it. The question you need to ask yourself is that, are you called into it? If you are called, the grace of God will be available to you to accomplish your roles or duties.

As an armour bearer, you need to know that your calling into this office is original and ordained to function as such without being distracted by other members or people around your mission. When you discover that your calling or mission is given to you by God, you become very positive and secured around some members of the church who may envy your office because you know that your mission can't be stolen because you are original and destined to serve in that capacity.

> "John answered and said, A man can receive nothing, except it be given him from heaven. Ye yourselves bear me witness that I said; I am not the Christ, but that I am sent before Him. He that hath the bride is the bridegroom: but the friend of the bridegroom, which standeth and heareth him, rejoiceth greatly because of the bridegroom's voice: This my joy therefore is fulfilled. He must increase, but I must decrease"

**John 3:27-30 KJV**

As an armour bearer to your leaders and your church or ministry, it is important that you know that your services or office is relevant to your leaders and your generation. Your contribution to the life of your leader and church has a generational effect on your society. Are you aware that you are not just occupying an ordinary position in your church?

You are very important and significant to your ministry. No matter what others have said about your ministry, you are indispensable and irreplaceable in your ministry or church. Remember that you are not an alternative and therefore your ministry makes the church complete. One thing I have never accepted within my ministry that I pray about daily is never to be an alternative; simply because having the mind-set of yourself being an alternative makes you develop a careless attitude. You also become less effective in your duties and your ministry.

In 2 Samuel 23:16, we were told that the three mighty men broke through the host of the Philistines, and drew water out of the well of Bethlehem, that was by the gate, and took it, and brought it to David. Do you know why? The three mighty men did not see themselves as alternatives. They saw themselves as relevant and significant in the life of David, the king. You are also relevant and significant in the life of your leader (**pastor, teacher, prophet, apostle and evangelist**). Church leaders are still praying for effective armour bearers who will dedicate their lives for the fulfilment of the work of God.

Be protective of your mission or your ministry to the point that you develop the attitude of a mother hen protecting her chickens. Never entertain people who will talk you out of your ministry. Learn to avoid people who will frustrate your ministry and make you very sad to the point of leaving your post. Be very passionate about your ministry especially when things are not going on well in your ministry. Get on your knees to intercede on behalf of the ministry to see the Kingdom and the purpose of God materialise.

In the life of Nehemiah for example, he had the mission to rebuild Jerusalem and that got him very upset. Bible recorded that he attacked the Jews standing in his way to prevent him from rebuilding the walls. In fact, he actually contended with them, cursing and smiting them for trying to be a hindrance to him and his ministry or mission (Nehemiah 13:25).

My fellow armour bearer, I am not advocating violence or fighting in your church against those who will stand in your way of ministry. However, you need to contend with them in prayer. Let your facial expressions show them that you are not in agreement with any negative behaviours.

### Men can only appreciate your efforts but God rewards your faithfulness and loyalty in service.

When you are called into the ministry of an armour bearer by God to your church, God is obliged to reward you. Please know that many are called but few are chosen into the ministry of an armour bearer. That is why many are falling along the side way because of some few challenges here and there but you who are actually called and ordained into it, you just flow and function happily because you are receiving heavenly backing and strength. Do not allow others make you unhappy because of the favour and the rewards you are getting for functioning in your office. You will always reap exactly where you have sown. Your ministry is ordained by God. So He is just rewarding your faithfulness and obedience. You cannot be denied your rewards.

Being faithful in your service, purpose, mission and ministry will attract God's blessing and promotions. "But without faith it is impossible to please Him: for he that cometh to God must believe that He is, and that He is a rewarder of them that diligently seek Him" (Hebrews 11:6).

Our Master and Saviour Jesus Christ got promoted after fulfilling his ministry here on earth and got rewarded in heaven (Philippians 2.5-11). Many armour bearers want to be elevated in life but do not want to sacrifice themselves by paying the price of servanthood.

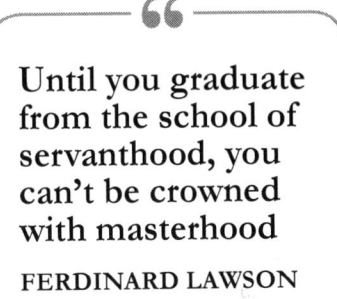

> **Until you graduate from the school of servanthood, you can't be crowned with masterhood**
>
> FERDINARD LAWSON

"For promotion cometh neither from the east, nor from the west, nor from the south. But God is the judge: he putteth down one, and setteth up another"

**Psalm 75:6-7 KJV**

## CONCLUSION

Service to a servant of God is service to God. This book reminds you that God has called each of you (armour bearer) to a unique service to your ministry especially in the lives of your leaders. Your unique service to your ministry cannot be possible without the grace of God to carry on serving faithfully.

We are empowered with special abilities to help build the house of God and to provide support to godly servants. He has put above us in leadership in order to fulfil and accomplish God's agenda for His churches and ministries.

Undoubtedly, we have been called to serve and it is very necessary that we understand and get deeper insight and into our ministry as armour bearers and the benefits await us in serving faithfully. Until we learn to appreciate, value and guard our ministry with great passion, loyalty, and involvement, we will not be able to be effective armour bearers. It is my fervent prayer that you live a fulfilled life in your ministry, run your race, serve with a servant's attitude so as to receive the heavenly prize for which God, through Christ Jesus, has prepared for your faithful service.

Go forward in grace.

Who is an armour bearer?..................................................................

What does it take to be an effective armour bearer?....................

Are you destined for the work of an armour beraer?....................

Are you born again? ........................................................................

Are you baptised and filled with the holy spirit?.........................

What are the duties of an armour bearer?....................................

Is the fruit of the spirit manifesting in your life?.........................

Define loyalty and faithfulness........................................................

How effective is your prayer life?..................................................

Can you mention some of the principles of an armour bearer andn?..................................................................................................

Are you happy in serving others?..................................................

# REFERENCES

**David O. Abioye**
Productive Thinking
Overcoming Stagnation

**Dr. David Oyedepo**
In Pursuit of Vision
Maximize Destiny
Exploit in Ministry

**Rhonda Jones**
You Must Change Your Mind to Change Your Life

**Mary Whelchel**
Defeating Discouragement

**Lester Sumrall**
Making Life Count

**R.W. Schambach**
What to do When Trouble Comes

**E.M. Bound**
The Weapon of Prayer

**Gordon Lindsay**
Prayer That Moves Mountains

**Keith Moore**
Servant Leadership in the Twenty-First Century

**Holly Spence**
Servant Leadership; the Heart That Serves

**Terry Nance**
God's Armour Bearer Volumes 1 & 2 Study Guide

**Nicholas Batzig**
Five Ways to Pray for Your Pastor

**Dr. John A. Tetsola**
Raising Spiritual Sons

# Prayer Guide for your Church and Pastor
## By Dr. Richard J. Krejcir

Use this prayer guide to pray daily for your church. Take one point each day of every month, and as you grow more in your discipline of prayer, double up by taking two or more.

First, praise God and thank Him for His blessings and goodness in all He has bestowed, even if you do not feel or see them. Remember your walk with Christ is all about Him working in and through us so your faith and love flourishes!

Day 1. Pray that we realise that our inheritance and hope as a church family is in God's incomparable and incredible great power which is available to us (Galatians 1:12; Ephesians 1:18-19; Philippians 3:10).

Day 2. Pray that our church, leadership and pastoral staff becomes more surrendered and poured out to Christ, so they can have spiritual breakthroughs by seeking the fear of God and the mind of Christ and the Spirit's leading (1 Corinthians 2:16; Galatians 2:20-21).

Day 3. Pray that your church and pastor have and continue to take hold a growing, consistent walk with Christ with a devotional life and prayer that is steadfast. Pray that they realise and allow Christ to work and use them as they grow closer in their faith, spiritual formation, maturity and love (Psalm 16:8-11; 73:28; Romans 8:31; 2 Peter 1:5-7).

Day 4. Pray that all of the leadership exhibit good Christian character and integrity with all of their relationships and dealings in life (Micah 6:8).

Day 5. Pray that your church leaders' and pastors' families will be cared for and respected and receive good consideration, so they can grow too, as they are usually misunderstood, under-appreciated, and ignored or overworked. Pray that all the staff be committed to their families with authentic love and care, that they will be strong and learn in the midst of trials, their homes a refuge and haven of rest and not be condescending or withdrawing from their own families (Psalm 91:9-15; Philippians 4:19; 1 Peter 2:23).

Day 6. Pray for discernment in exposing any plans of the enemy against our church or attacking our pastors and staff. Ask Christ to protect us as we wage spiritual warfare against the enemy on behalf of our church (Ephesians 6:11-12, 16; Colossians 2:6-8; 1 Peter 3:12).

Day 7. Pray for an increase of vitality, renewal and vision that is from God for the pastors and leaders personally and collectively so that the church can be galvanised then take a hold of, and then be revitalised as a caring, committed community for His Kingdom and purpose (Isaiah 61:3; Romans 12).

Day 8. Pray for the willingness and ability to authentically confess and repent of any wrong doing, false dependencies, misplaced ideas and loss of spiritual passion (Luke 13:1-3; Acts 2:38-39; Revelations 2:5-6).

Day 9. Pray that you and your church commit to follow the biblical mandate to support and encourage the leadership of the church (Ephesians 4:11-13; 1 Timothy 5:17-18; 1 Peter 5:1-2).

Day 10. Pray against gossip, negative criticism, false expectations, unhealthy burdens, strife and weariness that will seek to invade our church family (Psalm 91:5-6, 11; Luke 10:19; Ephesians 4: 17, 32-5:1).

Day 11. Pray that your church be a community of grace and forgiveness. That your church has an atmosphere of encouragement by being grateful for Christ's work in them that enables the congregation to be inspired to give genuine hospitality to all who come through your doors (Romans 15:4-6; 2 Thessalonians 2:16-17).

Day 12. Pray that your church commits to a healthy understanding, wisdom and accounting and handling of its stewardship and finances to better receive God's blessings (Proverbs 3:9-10; 1 Corinthians 9:15-18).

Day 13. Pray that your church and pastor will have the strength and endurance that they need to serve with excellence by the power of the Spirit and the support of the congregation (Philippians 4:13).

Day 14. Pray for healing, forgiveness and reconciliation for any misplaced expectations, criticism, ungrateful attitudes, flawed thinking, grief, hurts, and abuse (Isaiah 61:3; Mark 11:22-24, 2 Corinthians 10:3-5; Ephesians 4:32-5:1; Philippians 4:19).

Day 15. Pray that your church would receive God's direction and vision. That the congregation gets nourished from the substance of His Word and the needs of the congregation are met (Psalm 119:9-12; Matthew 18:20).

Day 16. Pray that our church becomes real authentic disciples of Christ who are learning, growing and making fruit and in turn making more disciples (Proverbs 19:23; Malachi 3:11; Matthew 28:18-20; John. 15:16; Galatians 5:22-23)

Day 17. Pray that the spirit and practice of humility is utilised and practised in and outside of your church, and that false humility does not take root (1 Peter 5:5-7).

Day 18. Pray that pride does not set in with our leadership and pastoral staff (Psalm 10:4; Proverbs 8:13).

Day 19. Pray that our church commits to place our focus on the supremacy of Christ and be dependent upon Him (Galatians 6:14; Colossians 1: 15-17)!

Day 20. Pray that our church and pastor give real biblical help and counselling from God's wisdom and Word to those in need (Isaiah 61:3).

Day 21. Pray that our church family will give Christ real authentic adoration, praise, impassioned worship and glory in private and collectively as a church. That worship is never to be a show, entertainment or talent focused, rather God is the audience to our praise (Galatians 6:14).

Day 22. Pray that our church and pastor take accountability seriously and each be protected and have people they are accountable to. Also, that each would cultivate and pursue healthy relationships (Galatians 6: 1-10; Ephesians 5:21).

Day 23. Pray that the Word of God will never be compromised, cheapened or dumped down; rather be delivered in confidence with power, conviction, clarity, boldness, with love and in truth (Acts 6:4; Colossians 1:28; 1 Timothy 2:1-2; 2 Timothy 2:15).

Day 24. Pray for discernment to seek God's leading and direction for the leaders and pastoral staff that they seek His ways and not trends, traditions, personal agendas or anything that is not from the Spirit and Word. Pray that they can discern and prioritise what is important and precious and what is not (Isaiah 6; 2 Corinthians 11:14; 2 Timothy 3:5; 1 John. 4:1; Revelations 4).

Day 25. Pray that God protects our church, leadership and pastoral staff from sin and misdirection and they have the wiliness and boldness to flee and confront sin (Proverbs 19:23; 1 Peter 1:16).

Day 26. Pray that we all draw near to Christ and seek holiness and His presence with more prayer (Acts 1:14; 1 Thessalonians 5:17; James. 4:7-8).

Day 27. Pray that we as a church family remain faithful and good stewards, so the financial needs are met (Psalm. 91:15-16; Philippians 4:19).

Day 28. Pray that negative thinking, stress, being overwhelmed, the ways of the world, the tyranny of the urgent, being overcommitted, over busyness, fatigue, compromise, pressures, overworked, underappreciated, misunderstandings, and stress to not get in our spiritual home and take over (John 14:1; Acts 6:2-4; 2 Corinthians 10:3-5; Ephesians 4:17).

Day 29. Pray that unity infuses your church so that your congregation is binding to Christ in love so the work of the Kingdom is promoted (2 Chronicles 30:12; Psalm 133:1; Romans 15:5).

Day 30. Pray that congregation is willing and able to come and support the church and staff with grateful hands and words. That you all realise that the pastors and leadership are necessary and called and accountable to God (Matthew 9:37; Acts 14; 1 Timothy 3:1-7, 10-15; 5:22-23).

Day 31. Pray that our church community commits to pray for our church, pastors, staff, missionaries, those in need, community and issues powerfully every day (Acts 1:14; 16:16; 1 Thessalonians 5:17).

And He cometh unto the disciples, and findeth them asleep, and saith unto Peter, What, could ye not watch with me one hour?

**Matthew 26:40**

0749038849

Printed in Great Britain
by Amazon